The Politics
of
Telecommunications
Regulation

Bureaucracies, Public Administration, and Public Policy

Kenneth J. Meier
Series Editor

Bureaucracies, Public Administration,
and Public Policy

The Politics
of
Telecommunications
Regulation

The States and
the Divestiture
of AT&T

JEFFREY E. COHEN

M.E.Sharpe
Armonk, New York
London, England

Copyright © 1992 by M. E. Sharpe, Inc.
80 Business Park Drive, Armonk, New York 10504

Library of Congress Cataloging-in-Publication Data

Cohen, Jeffrey E.
The politics of telecommunications regulation:
the states and the divestiture of AT&T / by Jeffrey E. Cohen.
p. cm.—(Bureaucracy, public administration, and public policy)
Includes bibliographical references and index.
ISBN 1-56324-050-5
1. Telephone—Government policy—United States—History—20th century.
2. Telephone—Government policy—United States—States—History—20th century.
3. American Telephone and Telegraph Company—Reorganization.
I. Title.
II. Series.
HE8819.C64 1992
384′.065′73—dc20
92-9815
CIP

Printed in the United States of America
The paper used in this publication meets the minimum
requirements of American National Standard for
Information Sciences—Permanence of Paper for
Printed Library Materials, ANSI Z 39.48–1984.

BM   10   9   8   7   6   5   4   3   2   1

To Laura

Contents

Tables and Figures

Tables

Figures

Foreword

The M. E. Sharpe series "Bureaucracies, Public Administration, and Public Policy" is designed as a forum for the best work on bureaucracy and its role in public policy and governance. Although the series is open with regard to approach, methods, and perspectives, especially sought are three related types of research. First, the series hopes to attract theoretically informed, empirical studies of bureaucracy and public administration. Public administration has long been viewed as a theoretical and methodological backwater of political science. This view persists despite a recent accumulation of first-rate research. The series seeks to place public administration at the forefront of empirical analysis within political science. Second, the series is interested in conceptual work that attempts to clarify theoretical issues, set an agenda for research, or provide a focus for professional debates. Third, the series seeks manuscripts that challenge the conventional wisdom about how bureaucracies influence public policy or the role of public administration in governance.

The Politics of Telecommunications Regulation: The States and the Divestiture of AT&T is an example of the highest-quality policy analysis conducted at the state level. It substitutes for simple theories of public policy more complex and more interesting explanations. It relies on a massive and time-consuming data-gathering effort that gives careful attention to measurement issues and provides a sophisticated empirical analysis to evaluate the utility of public policy theories.

Professor Cohen makes three major contributions to the literature on bureaucracy and public policy. The first is substantive. He documents the divestiture of AT&T and why decisions were made as they were. He does not exaggerate when he states that the breakup of

AT&T is the most significant antitrust event in U.S. history since the breakup of Standard Oil in 1911. As a result of divestiture, consumers were swept up in a massive economic experiment to decide who would pay for telephone service and how much each person would pay. The book documents how state governments chose between goals of equity and efficiency when deciding how to allocate the costs of telephone services among residential uses and business users.

The second major contribution of *The Politics of Telecommunications Regulation* is the specification of the role elections can play in the regulatory process. Consumer organizations frequently demand (as they did recently in California for insurance regulation) that regulators be elected, under the assumption that an elected regulator will be more responsive to consumer interests. Both observation (Oklahoma elects its utility regulators, yet they rarely make pro-consumer decisions) and systematic empirical studies, however, dispute this assumption.

Professor Cohen introduces his contingency theory of elections and public policy to specify the conditions under which elected regulators will produce decisions different from appointed regulators. Elections matter, he contends, when there is policy conflict along consumer/industry lines, when terms of office are short, when regulators are elected at-large from the state, when elections are competitive, when consumer groups mobilize, and when the institutional resources of the regulator are sufficient to influence policy. Using a pooled time series design, Professor Cohen tests his theory of elections and public policy and finds convincing evidence. Elections produce pro-consumer policies only under certain carefully specified conditions.

The third major contribution of *The Politics of Telecommunications Regulation* is the demonstration that bureaucratic capacity is a necessary condition for effective public policy. One area of promising research at both the national and state level is the examination of the capacity of bureaucratic agencies. If bureaucratic agencies do not have both resources and autonomy to use those resources, they rarely have impact on public policies, and policies generally tend to be less effective. Using his relative resources view of bureaucratic capacity, Professor Cohen adds an interesting dimension to this debate. He argues that it is not the *amount* of resources possessed by the bureaucracy that is critical, but rather its *relative* resources compared with those of other political actors. Using this theory, he documents the impact of bureaucracy as a means of translating electoral actions into public policy.

The Politics of Telecommunications Regulation provides an empirical base for discussions of state telecommunications policy. To make
significant advances in the study of public policy, similar policies are
needed in other areas. Professor Cohen has provided an excellent blue-
print for how such studies should be done.

Kenneth J. Meier
University of Wisconsin,
Milwaukee

Acknowledgments

Any book-length work incurs debts to those willing to read, comment upon, hear out, finance, and otherwise support the author. This project is no different. First, I want to thank those who read and/or commented on portions of this manuscript: Charles Barrilleaux, Greg Brunk, John Gates, David Nice, James Kuklinski, Michael Krassa. Two people read the entire manuscript, in various forms and versions, and thus deserve special mention: Barry Mitnick and Ken Meier. Further, I want to thank Ken for encouraging this project and including it in the series in which it now appears. I also want to thank the Ameritech Foundation for generously sponsoring this research with several grants under the auspices of their Ameritech Program at the University of Illinois–Urbana, Robert F. Rich, Director of the Institute of Government at the University of Illinois–Urbana, and Fred Giertz, Director of the Ameritech Program at the University of Illinois–Urbana, for their association with the Ameritech Program and for providing me with encouragement and support in conducting this study. I also want to thank the *Journal of Policy History* for allowing me to use material previously published in its pages and which now appears in chapter 1. Finally, I want to thank my family—my sister, my mother, and Laura—for their emotional support and love. They know only too well how many nickels have been spent on the telephone with them.

The Politics
of
Telecommunications
Regulation

Introduction

On January 8, 1982, the Department of Justice and American Telephone and Telegraph (AT&T) issued a consent decree, to which federal
Judge Harold Greene assented, that would implement the divestiture of
the world's largest private enterprise. Local and long distance telephone
operations were to be separated, and local operations were to be partitioned into seven regional providers, which would later become known
as the "Baby Bells." Moreover, the long distance provider, AT&T,
though still subject to Federal Communications Commission regulatory jurisdiction, would find itself situated in a newly competitive environment, one where other companies, primarily Microwave Communications Inc. (MCI) and Sprint, would also offer long distance telecommunications services. And the Baby Bells, like their progenitor, would
remain regulated under the several state public utility commissions
much as they had been before divestiture, only now the relationship
between local and long distance operations would not be so intertwined.

Not since 1911, when the Standard Oil Trust was dissolved, did a
federal decision have such an impact on such a large company. Like
the Standard Oil decision, the dogs of competition were unleashed in
telecommunications through the divestiture agreement. But unlike that
earlier decision, the AT&T divestiture also signaled a change in regulatory philosophy and policy: equity and universal access, the principles
of the regulatory regime over AT&T from the 1920s until the mid-
1980s, were replaced with a standard emphasizing economic efficiency.

Shock waves would reverberate beyond the corporate halls of the
one-time telephone giant and near monopoly. Relationships of customers to the telephone networks would be affected, the delicate interrela-

3

tionships among the many customer classes would be upset, and the political and economic alliances of telephone users, providers, politicians, and bureaucrats would be dissolved. All would require rebuilding and reshaping to meet the new environment. Policy subsystems that had been stable for upwards of 50 years were decomposing.

This book is about the policy reactions of the states to the divestiture of AT&T. The sheer magnitude of the divestiture alone recommends its study. Numerous studies of the decision and the events leading up to it have already seen print (Bickers, 1986; Coll, 1986; Derthick and Quirk, 1985; Evans, 1983; Henck and Strassburg, 1988; Horwitz, 1986; Kahaner, 1986; Kraus and Duerig, 1988; Stone, 1989; Temin with Galambos, 1987; Vietor and Davidson, 1985; von Auw, 1983). Surely more will come.

Relatively unique to my study, though, is its emphasis on policy responses. This is surely another justification for a new study. While much has been speculated about the effects of the divestiture, especially by economists (Kahn, 1984; Kahn and Shew, 1987; Kaserman and Mayo, 1986; MacAvoy and Robinson, 1983, 1985; Pool, 1984), little empirical research has investigated the policy implications of divestiture or the struggles of state policy makers to come to grips with it (but see Teske, 1990).

However, in the pages to follow, I hope to do more than merely study another interesting case or simply describe the new policy environment in the states. I hope to add to our understanding of the policymaking process by expanding upon a theory of policy making—a theory that emphasizes the importance of resources for influencing policy outcomes.

The guiding idea behind my theory is the notion that the impact of resources on policy making is conditional. Resources do not translate perfectly into policy impact or influence. There are two conditions that structure the translation process of resources into influence.

The first condition suggests that the impact of one policy competitor on public policy formation is conditional upon the resource levels of all other policy competitors. The second suggests that the impact of a resource is also conditional upon the efficiency of the flow of the resource from the influencer to the decision maker. Some flows are more efficient than others. Although other conditions also exist, I will demonstrate the importance, both in policy impact and on theory, of these two.

In the sections to follow in this introduction, I first outline briefly the policy problem that divestiture posed. Then I discuss the theory of conditional resource impact that is tested in later chapters. The introduction ends with a brief overview of the substantive chapters of this study.

Divestiture and Public Policy in the American States

The divestiture of AT&T not only upset the old corporate giant but also altered federal-state relations in the area of telecommunications, and by so doing, upset the balance of interests that had been so delicately equilibrated for the better part of the prior half century.

As I describe in more technical detail in chapter 1, the regulatory regime of roughly 1920–84 was built under a policy that emphasized equity and universal service over other possible goals. Universal service is a policy that offers telephone service to anyone who desires such service, and because the telephone began to be looked upon as a necessity of modern life by the early 1900s, universal truly meant everyone. Economic efficiency, the other possible policy course, is analogous to what we have now come to call "user fees." Economic efficiency argues that the best policy is one where the caller pays for the true cost of the call. If that cost is higher than the caller's utility or value for it, the call will not be made. Whereas universal service policy emphasizes the social benefits of telephone service, economic efficiency emphasizes economic impact, especially on telephone service providers, and relies on market mechanisms to implement the policy.

To institute the universal service policy, decision makers utilized regulation, rate averaging, and cross-subsidization. Importantly, a series of cross-subsidies were erected, whereby those either placing a higher value on telephone service (e.g., businesses and long distance users) or possessing greater resources to pay (businesses, urban users) were charged proportionately more for the service provided than the true cost of the service. These excess profits (or rents) were then transferred to others, primarily local users, residential users, and nonurban users, in the form of cross-subsidies.

Perhaps the most important of these transfers was from long distance users to local users. Facilitating this system was the fact that the cost of long distance operations decreased over time, so that, even though heavy long distance users were paying more for a call than its true cost, they still witnessed increasing economies as the system was modernized.

All of this came to a halt with divestiture. Subsidies of local operations were to be reduced and eventually eliminated. Long distance operations were now to charge only their true cost. Economic efficiency had replaced equity and universal service as national policy.

The problem for state policy makers, mainly the state public utility commissioners, was that for so long they had been able to build a cozy policy subsystem that was built upon federal government dispensation of long distance revenues to the states. With this long distance subsidy eroding, the localities would have to either find new sources of revenue to supplement these losses or lower telephone company operating costs.

Two possible policy solutions existed. One was to increase existing cross-subsidies at the local level (mainly from businesses to residents and from urban to nonurban areas) to maintain equity and universal service policy goals. The other policy solution was to follow the federal lead and jettison equity and universal service policies in favor of efficiency policies. This route would help local operating companies control expenses and operating costs. Either option required that someone in the local system bear the burden of the new policy course.

No matter which policy choice state decision makers opted for, conflict among the participants in the old policy subsystem would arise, and in all likelihood, the decades-old arrangement among them would dissolve. This book is about the policy options chosen and the politics of forging new alliances and coalitions.

To study state policy adaptations, I collected data on telephone rates in the jurisdictions where AT&T operated—the 48 continental states and the District of Columbia—for the period 1977 through 1985. In so doing, I focused on the ratio of business to residential rates, which captures one aspect of the business-to-residential cross-subsidy. Alteration of this cross-subsidy was to become one of the most contentious policy issues. Whenever issues of redistribution occur, and divestiture did require a redistribution, the deep pockets of business often become a convenient target. One may thus distinguish my study from Teske's important (1990) analysis of the adoption of economic-efficiency policies in the states. I am more concerned with the evolution of an existing rate structure, not the implementation of new rate arrangements.

Moreover, the time series component of my study allows me to look at policy as it evolves, not just to look at resultant policy. Three periods are captured during the 1977–85 time frame. The first is the pre-divestiture, old regulatory era of 1977–81. The second is the transitional era from divestiture's announcement until its full implementation, 1982–84. The third is the actual operation of the first full divestiture year, 1985. Time lags in the publication of needed data inhibited my ability to add more divestiture years into the data set. Still, the 1977–85 time frame allows me to capture the essence of the changes that divestiture wrought, as well the policy responses in the states.

As I demonstrate below, different states followed different policy courses, which were determined in part by the resources and influence of the participants in the policy-making process. Where economics might have dictated the nature of the policy dilemma for the states, politics determined the policy solution chosen. In the next section I present the theory used to explain the states' policy responses, which I feel can be applied to the policy-making process in general, and thus not exclusively to this case.

Notes toward a Theory of Influence in the Policy-Making Process

When studying public policy decision making, one is naturally drawn to the questions of *who* influenced the decision, by *how much,* and in *what ways.* Thus, the nature of power or influence is an integral part of the study of public policy decision making.

I begin by defining influence much as Dahl (1957, 1968) defines power (he equates the two): Policy influence is defined as the ability of actor A to move policy B to some desired state that without A's activity would not be attained.

Thus, to be influential, one must possess resources, but the impact of that resource base is conditional. In this study I focus on two of many possible conditions: the relative resource bases of all policy competitors and the efficiency of applying the resource base, that is, translating resources into influence. Hence, at its most basic level, any theory employing notions of power or influence must recognize and understand the resource base (Burns, 1978). Absent resources, influence is impossible, but as I demonstrate below, more resources does not automatically mean more influence.

Condition 1: Relative Resources

I begin the discussion of relative resources by building on the basic Dahlian definition of influence stated above. Such a definition is limited in that only one potential influencer is recognized. This definition might be useful for understanding dyadic systems, that is, where only one influencer tried to influence a decision maker. While simple in the abstract, the theory of interest group capture can be taken as a venerable version of such a view.

However, as is now well recognized even in the area of regulatory policy, for which interest group capture theory was originally developed, multiple influencers (or potential influencers) may be present and active, giving rise to the multiple interest theories of regulation. (We should caution against confusing *interest* with *interest groups*. Not only interest groups can be thought of as interests, e.g., mass publics, legislatures, executives; although, of course, interest groups clearly have interests to consider.)

In regulatory policy studies, multiple interest theories are now being developed and tested. For instance, the Gilligan, Marshall, and Weingast (1986) and Moe (1985) multiple interest studies are predicated on principal-agent notions. Inherent in the principal-agent paradigm is the idea that principals have some greater or lesser degree of influence over their agents, the degree of influence in part determined by the resources that the principal may bring to bear on the agent. In fact, one of the theoretical problems that theories of agency address is how the principal finds the slack resources and/or means with which to control the agent.

The recent work of Meier (1988) comes from a more classically public administration perspective. Meier views regulatory policy as being built in a subsystem where several actors compete for influence, with the success of their efforts in part a function of their resource levels. Meier is actually quite explicit about the importance of resources.

However, these versions of multiple interest influence are theoretically limited. They view final policy outcomes as a linear result of the resources of competing influencers. Thus, they tend to suggest that the more resources one possesses, the more influence one may have. While such a view may at first appear reasonable, I feel it is generally erroneous and at times might be misleading.

Again, let us refer to our basic definition of influence. Suppose A possesses four increments of resources and wants to move policy B east from where it now sits. Now suppose that influencer C possesses two increments of resources but wants to move policy B west. Based on the interactions of A's and C's influence, policy B moves only two increments east. C's influence in part countered A's attempts to influence policy. In effect, the influence of A on policy B is conditional upon both its own resource level and its competitor's resource level, in this example, C. Such a situation recalls the countervailing power theories of the pluralists (McFarland, 1987).

However, it is not the absolute level of resources that is crucial to influence, but rather the relative level of resources among competitors. For instance, now assume that A possesses twelve increments of resources, but C holds ten. Policy still will move only two steps, the same magnitude as the previous example, even though A holds three times the amount of resources as it did before and C five times its original level. Ironically, increasing C's resources by a greater magnitude than A's did not alter the relative policy influence of A or C on policy B. In both cases, policy moved two increments. If absolute resource levels were the critical factor, changing A's level by a factor of three and C by a factor of five should have narrowed the policy gap more in C's favor, but the policy gap remained stable.

One implication of this relative resources notion is that resource-poor influencers might have more influence over a policy decision than a resource-rich influencer when that rich influencer faces a rich competitor. Some substantive illustrations may be useful at this point.

Consider two bureaucratic agencies, the Defense Department (DOD) and the Small Business Administration (SBA). DOD may possess a stronger resource base than any other agency. Surely, few agencies can match DOD's resource base, its professionalism, employee base, and budget. In comparison, SBA's resource base is more limited. Its staff is smaller and less professionally oriented, and its budget is tighter.

An influence perspective that does not take into account the relative resources notion would predict that DOD should be more influential than SBA. However, the relative resources theory predicts just the opposite: SBA should carry more relative influence than DOD within their respective policy spheres.

DOD and SBA face policy competitors, for example, politicians with different resource bases. DOD competes with highly motivated politicians: those who not only possess a strong resource base, but who are also keenly interested in the substance of policy. We see this in the respective committees in Congress that oversee defense matters, as well as in the executive. Legislative oversight committees are well staffed, containing knowledgeable personnel. Moreover, key congresspersons also develop defense policy expertise. Examples include Senators Sam Nunn (D–Georgia) and William Cohen (R–Maine) and Representative Les Aspin (D–Wisconsin). Similarly, the staff of the National Security Adviser provides the president with independent and expert defense policy advice. And outside of the corridors of government, expertise and knowledge of defense policy matters can be found among the many defense contractors and defense think-tanks that dot the Washington, D.C., landscape. By no means does DOD monopolize the resources associated with making defense policy.

Matters differ when we compare the composition of the SBA's policy subsystem. The SBA faces legislators more concerned with the political and electoral implications of policies than their policy impact, and committee oversight staff are less professionalized than in the DOD case. Porkbarrel politics more than policy impact predominates in the congressional component of this subsystem. And the White House rarely is interested in SBA policy. Small business policy is not as salient as defense policy. It is often distributive in nature, and one requires little technical ability to determine program impact and recipient satisfaction levels. The SBA may possess more discretion and influence over policy design than various other bureaucracies, as long as it keeps one eye on providing political benefits to congressional politicians (Arnold, 1979).

Hence, we may suggest that the SBA has more impact over small business policy than DOD has over defense. Such statements, of course, require that we try to compare resources and influence across policy domains, something that is fraught with difficulty. However, while still crude, the comparison of DOD and SBA is instructive.

Moreover, any multiple interests analysis of policy outcomes requires an attempt at comparison of resources across actors, in this case, of legislative resources (e.g., staffing), gubernatorial resources (formal powers), interest group resources (size, wealth), and bureaucratic resources (expertise, staff).

However, as I will demonstrate, the relative resources notion produces some interesting hypotheses, proves statistically superior to its competitors, and thus pays off theoretically, despite crude measurement and analysis techniques.

Condition 2: Efficiency in Translating Resources

The first condition, that of relative resources, compares the resource base of policy competitors. However, that condition alone will not delineate fully the conditional nature of policy influence. The efficient translation of resources into influence requires that the resources of the influencer be able to affect the goals or aims of the policy maker. That is, the influencer must be able to affect the policy maker's incentive system, those rewards and punishments that the policy maker seeks or seeks to avoid. The more directly and completely the policy maker's incentive system can be impacted, the more efficient the translation of resources into policy influence.

Such a statement about translation efficiency seems self-evident. It becomes more theoretically compelling when the dictum is applied to a substantive problem. Many such problems exist. The one that I focus on in this book has important practical and theoretical implications beyond telecommunications and regulatory policy. It extends to the operation of democratic government in general: the impact of elections on policy making.

Simplistic theories of elections assume their policy efficacy, but considerable evidence suggests that elections do not always lead to policies that the electorate prefers. Cynics may suggest that elections are but hollow instruments anyway: the electorate is rarely keenly aware of policies and issues, politicians are quite adept at manipulating elections and the public for their own policy ends, and elections are more symbolically and ritualistically important than policy effective.

In the chapters that follow I take issue with this cynical interpretation, but neither do I wholeheartedly accept the "election-as-effective-policy-control-device" theory. Sometimes elections are effective in promoting public control over policy; sometimes they are not. More important than the mere presence of elections are the conditions under which they are held.

Thus, votes are more efficiently translated into influence when certain conditions are present. Specifically, I identify three conditions that are important before elections will be able to affect policy outcomes—

conditions that affect the nature and structure of decision makers' incentives and ability to produce public policies. Electoral arrangements and the degree of public mobilization affect incentives, while the institutional capabilities of the elected body will affect its ability to make and implement policy.

Electoral Arrangements

When barriers to easy reelection exist, policy makers may pay greater heed to public preferences. Two electoral arrangements may increase electoral threat: short terms and at-large elections. Similarly, electoral competition may increase election-day vulnerability. I focus on these three electoral arrangements in this study.

First, shorter terms may lead representatives to believe that members of the public can remember their decisions and that those memories may affect their voting behavior. Since the public possesses a short memory, the greater the time between elections, the less public constraint the elected decision-making body will feel. Time not only allows older decisions to fade from public consciousness, but past "incorrect" decisions may be corrected by decisions closer to the election date. Thus, elected bodies with longer terms of office may be composed of politicians with less of an incentive to produce policies that the public prefers than bodies offering shorter terms of office.

Second, the size of the constituency may affect the character of policy outputs. For instance, smaller aggregates of constituents, say in district systems, may allow special and minority interests and local parochialism strong voices in the decision-making body; whereas larger aggregates, like at-large systems, may force the decision-making body to address more closely the preferences of the majority.

Further, public concern and motivation to vote may increase as the size of the constituency increases. Electoral contests in larger districts may be more visible, and the public might think that it is voting for more important offices because more people are being represented. Moreover, this greater mobilization of voters may overpower special interests, which seem to have greater sway and impact in smaller constituencies.

Third, electoral competitiveness may affect the translation impact of voters' electoral resource. Electoral institutions placed in competitive environments often see high levels of turnover and members who are defeated for reelection. Politicians witnessing their peers suffering defeat may become keenly sensitive to public preferences and may impel their electoral decision-making body to produce policies that serve the larger class of voters. Lack of competition may insulate decision makers from public sentiments, thereby discounting the impact of the public on policy formation. Thus, we are likely to see competitiveness driving elected bodies to pursue policies that the public prefers.

To summarize, when terms are shorter, when districts are smaller, and when competition for office is keener, elections may more efficiently translate public preferences into policy influence.

Public Mobilization

A second major condition affecting electoral efficiency concerns how well the public is mobilized—how many people vote. Issues that mobilize the public or are perceived as mobilizing might motivate decision makers to produce policies that the public prefers. Actual or perceived high mobilization may affect policy outcomes by providing decision makers with information about public preferences, by voting into office candidates who are supportive of the public's positions and defeating those who are not, and by giving decision makers a ready explanation to interest groups for their inability to support a group's position on a certain issue—they, the decision makers, could not resist such strong public pressure.

Lack of public mobilization allows the decision-making body a freer hand when deciding policy directions and outcomes, whereas a mobilized public requires that political institutions attend to public concerns. Thus, when the public is, or is perceived to be, mobilized, or is perceived potentially to be mobilizable, decision-making bodies will be more likely to produce policies that the public prefers, and the efficiency of the electoral institution as an influence over public policy is heightened.

Institutional Resources and Capabilities

A third condition refers to the elected decision-making body's ability to make and implement policies. The body requires the institutional capability to be able to identify public preferences and translate them into public policies. For instance, Carmines (1974) argues that before a legislature can respond to public opinion it must possess the necessary institutional requisites that enable it to assess public preferences and convert those preferences into public policies, what he calls legislative professionalism.

An elected body might want to produce and implement such policies, but without the requisite resources, might not be able to do so. Thus, we must distinguish between the potential (desire) to produce policies that the public prefers and actually doing so. In effect, institutional capabilities affect policy production by increasing the institution's ability to assess public preferences and/or develop congruent policy options and by providing it with greater influence and control over the implementation process.

Summary

The study presented below provides statistical tests of these two ideas, relative resources and the conditional impact of elections on policy. To create the tests, I collected data on the resource bases of the active participants in the state telecommunications policy subsystem, the state public utility commissions (PUCs), telephone service providers, business and residential users, legislative committees and chambers, governors, and public interest groups. To test the election-related hypotheses, I also collected data concerning elected PUCs. These data were merged with the data on telephone rates to test the ideas presented herein. As I will show, strong support for both relative resources and conditional electoral impacts is found.

The Plan of the Book

This book is divided into two sections. The first section, comprising chapters 1 and 2, provides a historical overview of telephone regulation prior to divestiture. The second section, which contains chapters 3, 4, and 5, provides the statistical data and tests of the relative resource and conditional influence theories.

Chapter 1 discusses the road to regulation from the invention of the telephone in 1876 to the implementation of the full federal regulatory regime in 1934 with the creation of the Federal Communications Commission. Important theoretical elements that are utilized in subsequent hypothesis testing are presented. First, the ideas behind the competing equity–universal service and economic-efficiency policies are presented. They serve as a basis for understanding the nature of the policy debate during the era preceding divestiture. Second, I discuss the development of the multiple interests perspective by detailing in a historical fashion how the major participants came to be engaged in telecommunications regulation, their interests, and their basic resource bases.

Chapter 2 continues the historical discussion and brings it down to the 1984 divestiture. Chapter 2 particularly focuses on the debate over the contradiction between efficiency and equity. I show how federal policy was never completely committed to one or the other, and how the debate between advocates of each policy course led to divestiture. Moreover, I discuss in some detail the economics of telephone pricing to provide the reader with an understanding of how, during the half century leading up to divestiture, the alliance of disparate elements was forged into the state policy subsystems.

Chapter 3 begins the empirical analysis of the effect of the subsystems' participants on telephone rates. I identify strong impacts arising from many elements: legislatures, governors, public interest groups, and the public utility commissions, thus providing support for a multiple interest perspective. Startlingly, private interests, whom the venerable interest group capture theories focus upon, are found to have little impact.

Chapter 4 critiques the model in chapter 3 with the relative resources notion developed above. The relative resources theory of policy influence is compared with its major competitors, interest group capture and multiple interest influence. In all tests relative resources beats its rivals.

Chapter 5 looks at the conditional impact of elections on rate policy. Often a neglected topic, the impact of the public on regulatory policy and bureaucratic decision making became greater with the revolution in citizen participation at regulatory proceedings. Attendant with that revolution have been calls to elect regulators, with the hopes of increasing not only regulatory responsiveness to the public but accountability as well. The theory and analysis presented in chapter 5, however, find that simply moving to electoral recruitment might not affect policy outcomes. A conditional theory of election effects is offered, focusing on the nature of electoral arrangements, the mobilization of the public, and the institutional resources of the elected body.

All three are required to act in concert to promote responsiveness by elected regulators. Thus, it is necessary to discuss reform of the system, as well as theoretical implications.

Chapter 6 summarizes the findings, bringing together the themes of the substantive chapters. I close with speculations about what divestiture means for future policy in the information age.

1

Government and Telecommunications: Themes and Early History

Introduction

To understand the development of telecommunications policy in the states in the aftermath of the divestiture of AT&T in January 1984 requires an understanding of the structure of the telecommunications industry and the industry's relationship to government. This relationship has not been static. Over time it has changed and evolved. The sources of change are many—technological developments, theories of what constitutes the public interest, and the interests and preferences of players (Stone, 1989).

Our story begins with the founding of telephone regulation, focusing on AT&T—its aims and its relationship with government. As the story unfolds, the interests of other actors—business and residential telephone users and AT&T's competitors—enter. Once in place, the complex interrelationships among the various interests are revealed, setting the stage for an understanding of why divestiture happened and the reaction to divestiture in the states.

We can conceive of the telecommunications policy subsystem at this point in very simplistic terms that will allow us to begin to build a framework for understanding the government–industry nexus. The policy subsystem is always trying to reach a kind of stability or balance, whereby the interests and preferences of the government and the industry intersect. We begin with the major industry player, AT&T.

AT&T began as a profit-making enterprise, and has always desired profits. By controlling at least some of the market for communications, AT&T could protect some of its profit potential. However, markets are unsettling for competitors. AT&T, as a competitor with real or imagined (potential) competitors, sought ways to limit or restrict competition. In other words, AT&T sought to control and stabilize the market. With control established, profits could be secured, enhanced, and possibly predicted. Thus, the first dimension of our initial model is AT&T's preferences concerning control over and stability within the market for telecommunications. But throughout its history, AT&T had to justify its market share and profit motivation within a governmental regime that often changed. That, as we will see, was not always easy.

The second major player at this initial point is the government. The government acts as the guardian of the public interest. Conceptions of the public interest, however, may change over time. Primarily, two definitions of the public interest vie for policy supremacy here: social efficiency and equity. As we will see, these two states may be in a fundamental contradiction.

Social efficiency addresses the question of how much of society's resources will be spent in providing a service or product to its citizens. Ideally, efficiency affords high levels of goods provision at a low cost in the aggregate, but social efficiency does not address the distribution of goods and services, however fair or well balanced that distribution is. This, then, is the second important definition of the public interest in telecommunications: fair or equitable distribution of a product or service. The more a product takes on a public-goods character and/or the more the product is considered a requirement of life, the more public pressure mounts to ensure equitable distribution. A good discussion of the trade-offs between social efficiency and equity, discussed in terms of competition versus universal service, in the postdivestiture period can be found in Pool (1984).

Public goods are those that the members of society consume collectively, rather than individually (for instance, defense). Public utilities are often considered to possess a public-goods character. Utilities often define the infrastructure of a society and economy. Communications systems are often considered part of that infrastructure. Consumption or use of the telephone system requires two parties, the caller and the receiver of the call. Moreover, both parties must have access to all individuals on the system—thus, the public goods nature of the telephone system.

The conflict between social efficiency and equity derives in part from the differences in implementing them. Social efficiency requires a market implementation strategy. Only by allowing the laws of supply and demand to determine cost and investment can society provide a good at its most efficient level. However, markets are inherently unfair. Market mechanisms ensure that not only will there be winners, but also losers. Hence, governmental regulations are often used to ensure an equitable distribution. In effect, governmental regulations that promote equity try to reduce the number of losers. Such equity programs often lead to less than efficient provisions of services and goods, and in the process distort, if not hide, the "true" market price of the service or good. In democracies, equity policies are often popular. This is so even in nations such as the United States, which are committed to market capitalism, in part because of the size and impact of economic enterprises on the economy. When faced with such corporate giants as General Motors, IBM, or AT&T, the individual is likely to feel impotent. (On the ideology of capitalism and markets in the United States and their uneasy relationship with equity, see McCloskey and Zaller, 1984.)

In general, in the United States, social efficiency and equity are often juxtaposed. Popular culture and American economic theory argue that competition under free markets represents the best road to a socially efficient solution. Pro-competition policies have a long history in the United States, embodied especially in the Sherman Anti-Trust Act of 1890, and later in the Federal Trade Commission Act. While often called *regulations,* antitrust policies aim to ensure the proper functioning of the market. In contrast, equity policies, that is, regulation, aim to substitute government regulation for the operations of the market, which are thought to be imperfect and imperfectable.

As antitrust policy shows, there is a long history of government regulation of the economy. Some of the seeds were sown in the late 1880s with the implementation of the Interstate Commerce Act that created the Interstate Commerce Commission (ICC), empowering it to regulate railroad rates, routes, and practices. Government regulation of the economy matured in the 1930s under the policies and programs of the New Deal, and government regulatory powers were extended in the 1960s to cover social matters, as well as the traditional economic ones.

Government policy and preferences ride between two poles, with government control anchoring one end and unfettered competition the other. Along the government dimension of low to high levels of control, one can envision four ideal types of policies. At the extreme low end is *laissez-faire,* or no government control or involvement in the economy. This policy (or nonpolicy) maximizes social efficiency over equity. Also placing social efficiency over equity, but not so glaringly, is the next state, *antitrust.* In this state modest levels of government regulation occur, but to ensure a socially efficient outcome, not necessarily an equitable one. Equity begins to supersede efficiency in value at the next stage along the continuum, *public service* (or *utility*) *regulation.* Finally, in the fourth position, *nationalization,* government control is maximized in the name of equity. The government prohibits the market from functioning, asserting that equity is the only desirable goal for activities treated in this way.[1]

By crossing these two dimensions, government control over the market and AT&T's preferences for its level of market power, one can describe the nature of government–industry relationships.

Over time, the intersection of government policy and AT&T preferences has changed, because of (1) changing preferences along the government dimension, and (2) AT&T's (dis)satisfaction with its level of market power and security. The issue at hand for the government and AT&T is to reach a position that satisfies both. This has not always been easy or possible, and has often led to conflict between the government and AT&T. However, it is in the interests of both parties to find a mutually acceptable position because of the impact of both actors on each other and their desire for amicable relations.

We can now specify more fully the implications of equity and efficiency arguments as they relate to the provision of telephone communications. Social efficiency arguments suggest that society invests in the aggregate no more of its resources in a good or service than society can use. Surpluses are socially inefficient and wasteful, requiring more than necessary investment, while shortages are also looked upon as undesirable, as socially productive demand is not met. In the provision of telecommunications, this usually translates into consumers of telecommunications services being offered services and goods from providers in a competitive market whereby consumers can buy their desired type and level of service at the price they are willing to pay.

The problem with the social efficiency argument, according to the equity proponents, is that some goods and services might be required for everyone, but some might not be able to afford the service if they have to pay for it at the lowest level that a provider can offer it, that is, at its true market cost. This problem becomes even more severe when the value of the service increases as more individuals in society are added to the service. Therefore, society as a whole must redistribute, often in the form of cross-subsidies, whereby some pay more than the cost of providing the good to supplement others who cannot afford the service at its market cost. In telephone provision, this often means that business is charged more for service than consumers, and that urban areas pay more than rural areas. In the business–consumer situation, it is also assumed that business values telephone access more, hence it is willing to pay more for service. Thus, the equity argument often bases its pricing structure on "reasonable charges" and value of service pricing, whereas socially efficient pricing schemes use cost of provision to determine price. *Reasonable charges* is a term from regulatory policy that recognizes that regulated industries require a profit, but the profit should not be exorbitant—that is, it should be "reasonable."

AT&T as a profit-interested entity probably never really cared which government policy was adopted. However, as we will see, the equity regime for a very long time provided AT&T with a stable governmental environment that allowed it to pursue its profit and market interests successfully. The problem that AT&T was to encounter over its history was that the government instituted both socially efficient and equity-regulation policies at the same time, though locating them in different government bodies. This meant that AT&T's adoption of one governmental policy in pursuit of its market aims could come under fire when the government, or its parts, began to apply the other standard to AT&T. Satisfying one government agency could lead the other to become dissatisfied with AT&T's performance. In general, we will see that the Antitrust Division of the Department of Justice generally pursued an antitrust (social efficiency) policy, while the Federal Communications Commission generally pursued an equity-regulation policy. These jurisdictional conflicts and ambiguities over whether AT&T had antitrust immunity due to its regulated status formed one aspect of AT&T's problem with the government.

However, AT&T was not only reacting to governmental policy change. AT&T's actions and market position also led to changes in government policy preferences. Further, the behaviors of AT&T's competitors must be entered into the equation. Thus, there is a subtle interaction, and over time, mutual adjustment among all of these parties. This will be revealed as we examine the different periods in the history of AT&T from the invention of the telephone in 1876 to divestiture in 1984.

Periods in Telecommunications Industry– Government Relations

Most telephone historians identify three major periods or epochs of competition prior to 1934. There are a number of major histories of the period, all relying on roughly the same time scheme—the early period, 1876–80; the monopoly years, 1880–94; and the competitive period, 1894–1914 (Bickers, 1986, 4–30; Bornholz and Evans, 1983; Brooks, 1976; Coon, 1939; Danielian, 1939; Federal Communications Commission, 1938; Gable, 1969; Garnett, 1985; Stehman, 1925; Stone, 1989, 34–58). To these I add three more periods: the spread of regulation (1914–33), the regulatory period (1933–84), and the divestiture era (1984 to the present).

The first period spanned the earliest years of telephony, 1876–80, and was considered a period of unfettered competition. Government activity was generally nonexistent, except for patent protection. Bell's* main objective during these years was to protect its patents.

The next period, roughly 1880–94, was one of monopoly. During this period, government policy barely changed from the laissez-faire that characterized the earlier period. However, Bell moved toward a very secure competitive posture, monopoly control, which was based on its patent rights.

Those patents were to expire, leading to the third period, from the mid-1890s to 1914—one of often intense competition. Some divide the third period into two subperiods: 1894–1907 and 1907–14. The first subperiod was one of unbridled and often predatory competition. During this period Bell's competitive position declined, at times nearing a poor competitive posture, while government policy hardly budged.

During the second competitive subperiod, both Bell and the government changed their behavior and policies. Government policy began to move beyond antitrust, settling at regulation, though not reaching na-

---

*The corporation went through several name changes. I use "Bell" and "AT&T" interchangeably.

tionalization. Also, AT&T's competitive position improved during this second subperiod, in part because the company changed its policies regarding its competitors. AT&T began to trade off monopoly control of the market for a strong competitive position coupled with government protection of that position and cooperation with competitors.

From 1914 until 1933, the foundations of federally regulated monopoly were set. AT&T's competitive position remained strong, verging on dominant, but government policies were in flux, as proponents of antitrust, regulation, and nationalization began to compete for direction of government policy. The regulators won, but AT&T's relationship with the government would be plagued throughout the rest of its history as antitrust attacks periodically resurfaced.

The period from 1933 until divestiture in 1984 saw the implementation and demise of monopolistic regulation. This period was a reasonably stable one of government regulation and monopoly power for AT&T. However, the contradictions between antitrust and regulation were raised during this period, opening the door toward dissolution of the government–AT&T intersection of interests and leading to divestiture—the triumph of the antitrust proponents.

The divestiture period, from 1984 to the present, saw government policy structured such that some aspects of telecommunications policy were to serve social efficiency goals, while other aspects would serve equity ones.

The remainder of this chapter and the next detail the changes in government policy and AT&T's actions that led to divestiture. This will help set the stage for the empirical work to follow on state reactions to divestiture—the central focus of this research.

Early Periods of Telecommunications and Government Relations

Period 1: 1876–80

Soon after the invention and marketing of the telephone, Bell interests were threatened by the corporate giant Western Union. Western Union developed alternative telephone devices and challenged Bell patents in the courts, which Bell vigorously defended.

During the early years of telephony Bell defended its patents in some 600 lawsuits against various claimants (Herring and Gross, 1936,

47). In 1888, a case combining five patent suits against Bell reached the Supreme Court, and the Court, by a vote of 4 to 3, affirmed Bell's patent rights, thereby securing the patent strategy of the monopoly period (126 U.S. Reports 1. See Bickers, 1986, 13).

However, Bell as a fledgling company did not possess the capital resources to compete with Western Union, one of the largest companies in the nation. Competition raced along during these early years, but it appears that Bell's strong patent position, and Jay Gould's challenges to Western Union with his own telegraph network, led Western Union to back away from direct head-to-head competition with Bell. In a complex agreement, Bell absorbed Western Union's telephones, Western Union agreed to support Bell's patent rights, and the two agreed to divorce operations—Bell was to operate telephony exclusively, and Western Union would operate only telegraphy (Garnett, 1985, 44–54; Stone, 1989, 36–37). Thus, Bell's first contact with government came from patent protection, and that patent protection led to the creation of a monopoly.

This period, then, was one of market insecurity, but relative lack of government involvement. However, as Bell entered the next period, its market position improved, and the seeds of change in government policy also began to germinate.

Period 2: 1880–94

Bell's early years as a monopoly occurred as other industries were also in the process of monopolizing. During this time the public perception of the corporation changed, and this change was to plague the corporation throughout its history. Once considered the David that slew the Western Union Goliath, Bell was transformed in the public's mind into just another combine, an image that it would never shake, and that would in later years be symbolized with the name "Ma Bell."

During these monopoly years, Bell's financial situation stabilized, telephone equipment improved, long distance technology developed, and telephony diffused, but neither at the pace of the earlier competitive years nor at that of the next wave of competition. From 1877 (the second year of telephone marketing in the United States) until 1880 (the year of the accord with Western Union), the number of telephones expanded by 416 percent, or about 139 percent a year. Between 1880 and 1894 the pace of expansion, though still great, slowed to 33 percent a year. The reintroduction of competition in 1894 increased expansion rates to 78 percent a year from 1894 to 1907 (Garnett, 1985, 160–3). Gable (1969, 350) offers other figures but the same story of rising and falling expansion timed to the industry's competitive structure.

Still, during this monopolistic but unregulated era, laws of incorporation somewhat confined Bell interests. Bell initially incorporated in Massachusetts, an early state experimenter with regulation, especially corporate regulations (Holmes, 1890). These regulations sometimes impeded Bell's ability to capitalize and expand.

For instance, in 1879, Bell tried to increase its capitalization. To do so required state assent. In 1880, the state legislature allowed increased capitalization, but with restrictions and at a lower level than Bell sought. Further, legislative hearings also broached the subject of rate regulation, terrain that Bell did not want government entering (Garnett, 1985, 59–61).

In 1884, Bell again sought to increase capitalization. While the state legislature speedily passed the bill allowing it to do so, the governor vetoed it, arguing that Bell sought much more money than it required and that the state's public service commission should regulate Bell, as was the case with other utilities. Bell acceded to state regulation (which was corporation regulation, not utility rate regulation) and the governor agreed to increased capitalization, but at levels lower than Bell wished (Garnett, 1985, 103–5). In part because of these experiences in Massachusetts, Bell reorganized and reincorporated as the American Telegraph and Telephone Company in New York in 1896. New York state's attitude and policy toward business was more hospitable, which in part enabled Wall Street to become the business and financial center of the national economy at the turn of the century (Garnett, 1985, 105–6).

The move to New York illustrates AT&T's desire to maintain its monopoly position and to free itself of government restrictions. While these restrictions were not overly severe, except that they slowed the growth of the company, this was a period when government involvement in the economy was a new venture, and few knew what to expect. It was not until the end of the period that monopoly capitalists, first in the railroad industry, later in other industries, including telecommunications, saw the opportunity that government regulation presented. At this time, however, all that these monopolists saw were the costs of government regulation.

During this monopolistic phase, Bell was relatively free of governmental interference and exhibited steady, but comparatively slow, growth. One reason for Bell's conservative growth policies during this period was to prepare for the onslaught of competition that it expected when its patents would expire in the mid-1890s. Thus, although Bell created a monopoly during these years, the monopoly was neither secure nor permanent—it would expire when government patent protection expired. Bell interests would go through a rough period before learning that government protection in another form, regulation, could help protect the monopoly.

(Sub)Period 3a: 1894–1907

Two important developments occurred during the years between 1884 and 1907. One was that the idea of an integrated network from supply to service took hold at AT&T. The other was competition.

Vertical integration of the telephone network and the desire to offer end-to-end service can be viewed as the rationale behind the need for a monopoly. More cynical observers might view monopoly as the state that all capitalists desire. However, the logic of network integration in telecommunications is powerful, and in the future would lend itself easily to cooperation with the government in the form of regulation. Vertical integration involved AT&T providing itself with all that it needed from equipment to end-to-end customer service.

Further, as the value of telephone service was considered to be in part a function of the number of people connected to the network, the rationale and incentive for long distance operations developed. However, to ensure that a long distance network could be built and that the local companies could interconnect with it, centralized control was required. Hence, during this period AT&T began to control the operations and standards of the locals, thereby ensuring compatibility and cooperation among them. An integrated network, which reduced transactions costs among interacting components and created uniform standards of operation and service, was built and would become a mainstay of corporate ideology until the divestiture threat of the 1980s (Garnett, 1985; Langdale, 1978; Smith, 1985; Stone, 1989, 38–39, 69–71).

Competition came swiftly to AT&T after its patents had expired, and while one would expect AT&T's control over the market to decline, it seemed to decline more precipitously than expected. By 1900, barely six years after the patent expirations, almost one-third of the market was owned and operated by nonconnecting, non-Bell companies. These nonconnecting competitors peaked in market share by the early 1900s with about 40 percent, but Bell-owned telephones as a percentage of the market declined until about 1910, when Bell's share of the market dipped below 50 percent (Garnett, 1985, 160–63).

Independent telephone company competition met AT&T head on, often competing directly in AT&T markets. According to Herring and Gross (1936, 61): "[I]n almost every city in which Bell exchanges existed, rival exchanges were established by independent companies." These rivals hoped to feed on dissatisfaction with Bell services and rates. Expansion of the independents also ventured into areas untapped by AT&T, the small towns and rural communities of the nation. In these more agrarian areas, the independents became powerful rivals to Bell.

The major history of the independent movement is MacMeal's book (1934), but the MacMeal study was financed by the Independent Telephone Association, and hence is self-serving. One very good study of the structure of competition between AT&T and the independents, as well as among the independents themselves in the years between 1900 and 1917, is Barnett and Carroll (1987). They found that the noncommercials exhibited a mutualism structure—that is, their fortunes were tied together as a group (the death and survival rates of *mutual companies* were related). *Commercial companies,* Bell and the larger urban independents, competed vigorously with each other. Furthermore, a symbiotic mutualism existed between the commercials and the mutual companies, as little competition was evident between these two market segments.

Gable (1969, 345) reports figures on the extent of head-to-head urban competition between Bell and its independent rivals. In 1902, of 1,051 cities of over 4,000, 1,021 had telephone service. Of those, 414 (41.3 percent) were served by Bell exclusively, 137 (13.7 percent) were the exclusive territories of the independents, and 451 (45.0 percent) were served by Bell and at least one independent. Thus, even in its core market—urban areas—Bell faced strong challenges by the independents.

An early Census Bureau report provides figures on the expansion of the independents' movement and its penetration as of 1907, the earliest year such figures are available on a state-by-state basis. Regionally,

AT&T and its affiliates were strongest in New England, with 89.3 percent of the telephones in that region in 1907. Its other areas of greatest market control were the mid-Atlantic states, the Pacific states, and the mountain states (mostly Colorado), where AT&T controlled 70 percent of the market or better. In the southern states, AT&T usually controlled about half of the market, but it was in the midwestern states where the independents were strongest. For instance, in the west/north-central plains states (Iowa, Kansas, Nebraska, Minnesota, the Dakotas, Missouri) the independents controlled over three-quarters of the telephones, and in the midwestern states of the Great Lakes area, the independents controlled almost 60 percent of the market (Bureau of the Census, 1915, 35–36).

One factor accounting for this regional distribution was that though the midwestern grain states were relatively affluent, their population was sparsely settled. AT&T preferred controlling urban areas, for which the cost of service provision was lower and traffic was greater, leading to greater potential to recoup investment. However, the relative affluence of the midwestern states created a great demand for telephony. This is contrasted by the South's experience: AT&T gained entry into the urban South relatively easily and often with the support of state governments, which tried to promote telephony's expansion; but the rural South was so desperately poor that the independents, though valiant, were not very successful in penetrating these areas (Lipartito, 1988, 1989).

The rest of the market was controlled by non-Bell companies that connected to Bell. Connecting non-Bell telephones to the Bell network represented a change in policy at Bell, which President Theodore Vail instituted in 1907. It also represented a policy change among some of the independents, many of whom had contracts and licenses expressly forbidding interconnection with Bell. As we will observe, this new AT&T policy was important in the larger aim of creating market stability. Coupled with regulation, it would provide a secure market for AT&T for generations.

Most striking about AT&T's pattern of market loss was the fact that competition was generally based on getting into a market first. Most competing firms felt that getting into a market would preclude competitors from entering because of the capital costs of building networks, laying lines, and securing rights-of-way. And as the value of individual subscription to the service was based on how many other people also subscribed, late-entering competitors were disadvantaged—they could not offer subscriber lists comparable to those of earlier service providers. Finally, many cities offered exclusive franchises to the telephone companies, often precluding entry of competitors within their territory under some arrangements.

Still, price competition, though not a policy, did occur. In many cities where both independents and AT&T operated, the independents offered lower rates, but often with disastrous results. These companies began with less money behind them—price competition often led to poor service and maintenance, and, ultimately, bankruptcy (Herring and Gross, 1936, 61–62).

Prices declined greatly during the competitive era. Between 1894 and 1909, Bell's prices for businesses and residents in competitive areas dropped by 47.5 percent and 64.9 percent, respectively, and its prices for businesses and residents in noncompetitive areas declined by 47.1 percent and 57.6 percent, respectively (Gable, 1969, 346). While competition clearly had impact on prices in competitive areas, the threat of potential competition may have depressed prices in noncompetitive areas. Added to competition's direct price effects was the impact of innovation and product development on prices. More efficient, better equipment reduced the costs of operations, which could be passed on to the customer. It is likely, too, that competition inspired these innovations.

The independents' major weakness, though, was the lack of a long distance network. Realizing this and also feeling that pooling their resources would enable them to compete with AT&T on a more level playing field, an organization of independents, the National Association of Independent Telephone Exchanges, was created in 1897. Its major goals were the union of independent telephone companies, the establishment of a long distance network, and united resistance against AT&T (Herring and Gross, 1936, 63). United action among the independents seemed to work so well that in 1909 a merger of independent telephone companies was planned with an initial capitalization of $100,000,000, a huge sum for its day (New York Times, 11 July 1909, 3). Not surprisingly, AT&T charged that such capitalization was excessive and that AT&T alone could offer all the requisite telephone service that the nation required (New York Times, 15 July 1909, 9).

Competition not only depleted AT&T's market share, but it drained the company coffers, as well. Large debt financing came to AT&T in

1902. In 1901, Bell debt amounted to $15 million. By 1906 it had ballooned to $128 million (Garnett, 1985, 117–18). The policies of the early period of competition (1895–1907)—patent purchases, expansion, and refusal to interconnect and/or sell to competitors—gave way to a new set of policies that included product development, absorption of competitors, interconnection and sales to competitors, and regulation (Gable, 1969, 349–56).

The rapid pace of competition, AT&T's eroding position, and the uncertainties of municipal regulation all led to the giant's acquiescence and support for monopolistic regulation. However, AT&T's flirtation with regulation was tentative at first. Yet, AT&T sought a way to protect its market position. The policy of free market competition was sapping the company, as it had done to the railroads 20 years earlier.

Government was also beginning to change its attitude about the telephone industry. A telephone began to be viewed as a necessity of life, a public utility that all should have. Thus, the first rousing of a public interest equity argument appeared, challenging the older prevailing idea that social efficiency in the provision of telephony was best.

(Sub)Period 3b: 1907–14

By the early 1900s, public forces began to alter the long-standing governmental preference for laissez-faire. A number of policy options existed, including regulation and nationalization. In this section I address the question of who supported and opposed the various policy options and why. The debates illustrate how the differences between social efficiency and equity affect policy choices.

A full complement of interests can now be identified: consumers, businesses, independent telephone companies, AT&T, and the government, each seeking a solution to its telephone problem. Our theoretical framework is more complex than early public interest theories of regulation or simple interest group capture theories (Mitnick, 1980, 84–154). Rather, our framework has more in common with the multiple interest approach (Gilligan, Marshall, and Weingast, 1986). However, as I will show in the following chapters, the interests, preferences, and resources of government officials also have important implications for policy making, something not considered in the multiple interest model.

Government is not a monolith. In telecommunications policy, the dual level regulatory system presents state and federal regulators with different incentives and interests. And even at the federal level, the FCC and the Department of Justice adhered to two different regulatory policies through most of the regulatory period (1933–84), in part because the resources and missions of the two agencies differed. However, at this juncture, we are concerned only with the actors outside of government. In the early 1900s, the federal government and most state governments had not developed an active policy regarding telephones. Indeed, government was just deciding whether to engage a telephone policy.

Consumers

Consumers almost always favor policies that promote equity over social efficiency. (In fact, in the deregulatory environment of the 1970s and 1980s, I would argue that it was big business, not consumers, who were the prime supporters for deregulation.) Consumers usually feel that their interests are better served by equitable distribution than by social efficiency. Social efficiency policies often disadvantage many consumers. Further, in modern democracies, the equity argument tends to be quite potent, and is a major weapon that public figures and demagogues use to mobilize the public. Thus consumers tended to prefer either regulation or nationalization of the telephone. However, the generally pro-market ethic of American culture is not a hospitable environment for nationalization policies. Therefore, consumer preferences tended to settle on the regulatory option.

A number of conditions in telephone service at the time seemed to breed fairly broad public support for regulation. Three issues were primary: rates, complaints, and service.

Many consumers felt rates were too high. This seems especially to be the case in areas where monopolies were providing service. For instance, consumers in New York City noticed that telephone rates were lower in neighboring Brooklyn in 1909. Brooklyn was served by an independent company trying to gain entry into the New York City market, which the AT&T subsidiary, New York Telephone, served. By offering lower rates, the independent hoped to convince the public and city officials to allow it entry into the market. (Much of this discussion and that to follow is based on an investigation of telephones by the

New York state legislature in 1910. See State of New York, 1910 and Mosher, 1935.) Consumers wondered why the independent could offer low rates, while the government would not force New York Telephone to follow suit: consumers felt that New York Telephone was charging monopolistically high prices.

However, public reaction was somewhat ironic. Evidence cited on page 29 suggested that competition between AT&T and the independents did lower rates, as economic theory would predict. Further, consumers often felt that competition had a depressing effect on rates. A survey of 1,300 consumers in 189 cities in the early 1900s found that over 90 percent felt that rates by both Bell and independents were lowered by the introduction of competition from the independents (MacMeal, 1934, 168–69). However, we do not know how scientifically the sample was drawn. Hence, public preferences for either regulation or government ownership, the two most prevalent public positions, may be somewhat at variance with the complaint about rates, at least among these urban residents.

Aside from rate complaints, consumers felt that the monopolistic telephone companies were not accountable. Routinely, telephone companies did not offer itemized billings. When consumers complained about possible overcharges, telephone companies delayed resolution of the dispute. Customer refusal to pay until the problem was settled often led the telephone company to disconnect service. Hence, people wanted some kind of regularized system where they could make a complaint without fearing company retribution.

Wiring of cities was also a problem that concerned consumers. Early urban pole wires were iron and were strung above-ground, often over people's yards, along with electric power and other lines, presenting a crazy-quilt pattern. Wiring was unprotected and often was downed due to rust, weather, and sometimes fire (which could be caused by telephone and power lines touching). This led some municipalities to require underground wiring, but it was not until the mid-1910s that suitable insulation and pulled copper wire were available, lessening this danger. Thus, these wires caused safety, as well as aesthetic, concerns for consumers.

Business

The complaints of business resembled those of consumers, but they were probably more intensely voiced. While both business and consumers valued adding people to the telephone network, business had a greater stake in expanding the lists of subscribers. Doing so increases the number of people whom business could contact or be contacted by, and as it found telephony to be a boon, as well as a more efficient way of conducting business, complete subscription lists were highly valued. (This is little more than a restatement of the comparative value of telephone connections to business and consumers. Long-standing regulation has understood this comparative valuation and accordingly charges business more for telephone service than it does consumers.)

The competition of the 20 years subsequent to the expiration of the Bell patents affected business. Competition meant that business would have to subscribe to both competing telephone services when competition existed locally. Many businesses felt that they were thus doubly charged, and such *perceptions* of overpayment fueled resentment toward the telephone companies (Gable, 1969, 348). However, as noted above, it is not clear that multiple subscriptions increased costs to business, because of the price-dampening effects of competition. What was important for the political climate, though, were these perceptions. Business preferred a system that would require interconnections between telephone systems or provide for some sort of intersystem integration, thereby allowing business to attach to one company and receive the benefits of connection to all subscribers. Two policy options could fulfill the needs of business—nationalization and regulation.

Business tended to oppose nationalization, though. Setting an example of nationalizing one industry might lead to nationalizing others. Rather, there existed a confidence in business and in the ability to apply business methods to government—regulation by an independent, bipartisan commission was the preferred solution of these "progressive" businesses.

Thus, business held policy preferences similar to those of consumers. It might be best to consider both as one group—telephone users with preferences for some form of equity arrangement rather than social efficiency. In fact, some people did not feel that social efficiency could be obtained through competition. They considered telephony to be a natural monopoly, arguing that natural monopoly conditions rendered competition less socially efficient than other mechanisms—for instance, regulation. Hence, some form of government control could attain both a more socially efficient and a more equitable solution than could the competitive status quo.

The Independent Telephone Companies

In general, the major opponents to regulation were the major opponents of AT&T—the independent telephone companies. The independents' resistance to regulation was based in part on a fear that regulation would freeze them and Bell at their then-current status. As Bell enjoyed market superiority, regulation would governmentally sanction that superiority long into the future.

Further, as the independents were expanding so greatly and so rapidly, they naturally felt that their market share could expand as well. From 1895 to 1905, nonconnecting independents grew rapidly (1885–1900: 313 percent per year; 1900–1905: 44 percent per year). In contrast, Bell grew at a slower rate (1895–1905: 34 percent per year; 1900–1905: 35 percent per year). From 1895 to 1907, AT&T added 2,703,009 telephones to its systems, the nonconnecting independents added 2,249,578, and the connecting independents added 826,489. Together, the combined independents surpassed Bell's total additional telephones. Thus the rate and accumulation of telephones led many of the independents to believe that they could surpass Bell and overtake the mammoth corporation.

The independents also thought that AT&T was vulnerable in other respects. Not only were they competing successfully against the giant, but they watched AT&T absorb great debt financing to stave off their competitive threat. Further, the counterorganization of independents, first into associations, then into protocombines, and finally into a planned interstate merger that would rival Bell's resources, made many of the independents heady with the possibilities. (Turning into another combination would, however, undo the structure of the independents, which was built on small, locally owned and operated companies. However, to match AT&T's resources, many of the small companies were already merging or pooling by the early 1900s.)

We get a very good sense of the attitudes of the independents from this exchange between a president of a Brooklyn-based independent and the Joint Assembly-Senate state legislative committee that toured New York state in 1909 investigating the telephone and telegraph companies of the commonwealth (State of New York, 1910, pp. 277–78).

> Q. Do you think that if your company installed its system in the city [New York] that you could reach that 25 percent of the people south of Fourteenth Street?

THEMES AND EARLY HISTORY 35

A. Yes, I think we could reach a very large proportion of them, and under the plans that we now have outlined—our policy rather—I think we could practically force the use of our system in practically all of the business houses in New York.

Q. That is, you would have your telephones in 100 percent of the business places south of Fourteenth Street?
A. We should make an effort. We might succeed.

Q. You think you could accomplish that?
A. We think we could force it in order to protect the business interests.

Q. What effect would that have on the business of the New York Telephone Company [an AT&T company] in that territory?
A. That would force them to meet our rates and furnish equally satisfactory service or they would gradually recede as we progressed with our installation.

Q. So that eventually they would be forced out of business as you accumulated business?
A. Well, that is a rather strong statement to make here, though there have been a number of places where that has been accomplished in quite large territories.

Q. So that if that happy result obtained here, you would then have the field to yourselves so far as the lower end of the island [Manhattan] is concerned?
A. Well, so far as the whole island is concerned.

Q. So far as the whole island is concerned?
A. Providing we met the entire satisfaction of the public.

Q. And if that time should arrive, then the people of New York City would find that they have exchanged one monopoly for another.
A. Well, we haven't crossed that bridge yet.

Q. You are willing to, I suppose?
A. We are willing to approach it.

Rarely does one find a monopolist so honest about such intentions.

The independents were not completely united on this matter. They were highly decentralized, and the various companies perceived different conditions and prospects. In 1910, Frank H. Woods, president of the national association of independents, suggested that they change their policy prohibiting interconnection with Bell and enter into a system that would legally supervise the relationship between the independents and Bell, preferably by the Interstate Commerce Commission (MacMeal, 1934, 183).

One reason for this change in the attitudes of important leaders of the independents was the realization of Bell's superior resources, which were enhanced when the Morgan banking interests began to take over AT&T around 1907, and the weakness of the association of independents, which had no power to force member cooperation and pooling of resources to build a competitive national network. Competition among the independents plagued them as well (Bickers, 1986, 18).

Thus, by the end of the first decade of the twentieth century, cracks in the wall of independent opposition to regulation began to appear. Also, AT&T's policies changed—the giant corporation began to interconnect with some of the independents on a case-by-case basis and also began to absorb some by purchasing them. The accommodation of AT&T to some independents and AT&T's purchase of strategically located independents weakened the cumulative resources of the independents and their resolve to contest with AT&T.

In the early years of the twentieth century, the aggressive, expansionist, and successful independents were not ready for regulation and certainly opposed nationalization. Nor did they prefer the laissez-faire status quo. Instead, they preferred antitrust, which would give them a weapon to use against Bell, a weapon they would invoke, though with only minimal success, as Bell countered with a regulatory strategy and a well-designed publicity campaign to mobilize public support for regulation (Long, 1937a, 1937b, 1962).

AT&T

AT&T's position with regard to government is surely the most complex. Of the four possible policy options, laissez-faire, antitrust, regulation, and nationalization, AT&T preferred regulation.

Nationalization. Clearly, the profit-motivated capitalists that ran the company did not want to see their highly profitable enterprise nationalized, but nationalization sentiment existed. As early as the turn of the century, critics of telephone companies were calling for nationalization

(Clark, 1892; Judson, 1914). These critics often charged that rates were higher in the United States than in European countries, where government tended to own the telephones. They also charged that service in the United States was poorer and that the government could operate the system more efficiently and in a less costly manner because it would not be in the business of making money. Further, they suggested that service would be provided to areas that did not appear profitable enough to receive service. Eliminating competition would also eliminate the waste that duplication of service and plant created. And finally, they argued that telephone service was similar to mail, but it differed only in that it was spoken as opposed to written.

While various government officials had offered proposals to nationalize the telegraph in the years between 1867 and 1873, none were taken very seriously. However, with the rise of the progressive movement and its belief that government could bring the principals of business and scientific management to government administration, the idea of operating all of the electronic communication media through a civil service operation began to gain credence and some support.

This culminated in a major report by Postmaster General Albert Sydney Burleson in 1913 that argued for the postalization of both the telephone and telegraph. (Portions of Burleson's report can be found in Judson, 1914, 115–19.) Burleson was not the first postmaster to suggest that the telephones be regulated. Taft's Postmaster Hitchcock did so, but Burleson's report was taken more seriously. The Burleson report was based on the statistical comparisons of rates and services between the United States and European nations with public ownership of the telephone.

On December 13, 1913, Representative David John Lewis of Maryland read into the *Congressional Record* a long report arguing for the absorption of the telegraph and telephone into the Postal Department, relying on data similar to Burleson's. (It is reprinted in full in Judson, 1914, 41–87.)

Furthermore, a committee of the Post Office department conducted research on the question of postalization (Judson, 1914, 88–114). It is quite well documented and relies heavily on statistical comparisons of rates and service between the United States and nations with government ownership of the telephone.

Thus, credible sources with some influence within the government began to press earnestly for government ownership on the eve of the

First World War. Further, the fact that such proposals came from the Wilson administration, which had a reputation of progressivism and an ability to get its program enacted by Congress, heightened the prospects for nationalization. Although President Wilson personally did not support nationalization (Judson, 1914, 166–67), the fact that it was being debated in his administration surely affected the opinion climate, prospects for nationalization, and AT&T's behavior. And this mounting pressure on AT&T may be one reason that it entered into the Kingsbury agreements with the federal government in 1914 (to be discussed in a later section).

Nationalization and the Burleson report were not wholly accepted. One eminent scholar of the period criticized the methodology of the statistical comparison used in the study (Holcombe, 1914; also Unsigned, *Journal of Political Economy*, 1914). Reports in the popular press were also critical (Bethel, 1914; Brooks, 1914). One of the more scathing attacks claimed that Burleson was just trying to gain added patronage for the Post Office Department. Upon his coming to office, he had replaced the 16,000 Republican postal employees with Democrats. Civil service had not yet covered the Post Office (Unsigned, *Saturday Evening Post*, 1914). And as expected, AT&T entered the public attack, criticizing Burleson on grounds of logic, economics, and fact (American Telephone and Telegraph, 1914).

Still, the specter of nationalization was present and gaining momentum. This fact is often lost on historians of telephony during this era (but see Bickers, 1986, 23). As we will see, Bell's acceptance of regulation was in part motivated by the desire to avoid harsher forms of government control.

Parenthetically, the federal government experimented with nationalization during the First World War. During this time AT&T officials ran the company under the direction of Postmaster Burleson. AT&T cooperated with the government's war efforts, but disputes arose over rates. Soon after the war ended, AT&T reverted back to private control. While not a failure, government nationalization never again surfaced as a policy option (Bickers, 1986, 24–25; Brooks, 1976, 150–51, 156–57).

Antitrust. Bell's entire history until divestiture can be thought of as an attempt to evade the antitrust laws. Bell showed its antipathy to the antitrust conception during its monopoly period by strongly defending its patents and by purchasing other patents to preclude competitors from legally entering the telephone communications market. The first significant antitrust law, the Sherman Act, was passed in 1890, shortly before the expiration of the Bell patents. As Bell faced stiff competition in the first decade after the patent expirations, the Sherman Act had little relevance to Bell. However, upon the accession of Theodore Vail to the presidency of the company in 1907, with the support of the Morgan banking interests, Bell began a strategy of beating the opposition by purchasing them. Such a policy clearly affronted the intent of the Sherman Act. Thus, Bell was clearly no friend of antitrust. This early behavior would haunt the company throughout its history, and even with a record of good public service during the era of regulation, suspicions about Bell's monopolistic ambitions endured.

Antitrust acceptance would also weaken Bell's market position—a major reason for Bell's antagonism and disregard for such policies. In later years, Bell would create a company ethic of public service, one that included equitable distribution of telephone services, thereby building an organizational structure that viewed antitrust and its attendant policy of social efficiency as threats, feelings that would last until divestiture.

Regulation. Since three options, continuation of laissez-faire, nationalization, and antitrust, were abhorrent to Bell interests, Bell reconciled itself to government control through regulation. Bell thus hoped to maintain its market position under government protection and fend off attackers that would nationalize or use antitrust laws against the company. Of the different varieties of regulation, Bell preferred the commission form (directed by the states) to federal regulation. At the time, regulation tended to be of the municipal variety, something Bell also sought to evade.

Municipal regulation was often less than optimal to both the localities and the telephone companies. First, municipal boundaries did not always follow telephone company boundaries, which meant that companies would be regulated by more than one municipality or that only a part of its operations was regulated. The movement by AT&T to consolidate and purchase its own affiliates in the mid-1900s led to AT&T's support for statewide oversight.

Further, municipalities had the power only to grant franchises to companies to operate telephone service, though in some instances maximum rates were identified in these regulations. Cities found that their franchise contracts were poorly drafted, partially because city officials lacked expertise. Another source of poorly drafted contracts was corruption. Bribery of local officials was endemic in urban areas at the time, which surely affected the awarding of telephone franchises and cast public doubt on the intentions and image of the telephone companies. These problems limited municipal regulation as a solution for AT&T's woes, because such regulation would not solve AT&T's market problem with the independents, nor would municipal regulation quell calls for nationalization (Mosher, 1935).

Also, since franchises took on contractual obligations, the terms of agreement could not be altered unless both parties agreed. Long contracts were immune to economic tides, sometimes benefiting consumers and sometimes benefiting the telephone companies. To keep from being locked into unfavorable franchise terms, cities could require nonpermanent contracts, a source of uncertainty for the telephone companies, who might find their franchise going to a competitor after expiration. (Good discussions of the limitations of franchises in general and municipal regulation in particular can be found in Holmes, 1915, 298–310, and Mitnick, 1980, 29–30.)

Moreover, there existed several examples from the electric utility industry where locals municipalized companies. Finally, local control of the telephone companies often became a political football beyond the ability of the telephone companies to deal with effectively. State control, it was assumed, would take some of the blatant partisan politics out of telephone regulation, thereby making state regulation a more preferred option (Holmes, 1915, 304).

Compared with state regulation, federal regulation in 1910 was also less of an option, though there is little indication that AT&T opposed it. Interstate communication played little part in telephone operations of the day. Therefore, federal regulation would have little impact on regulation of the industry. For instance, as late as about 1930 Bell estimated that in its exchange service, 0.47 percent of its messages were interstate, the rest intrastate. Of its toll service, 19.5 percent of messages were interstate. Of all services, only 1.36 percent of messages and 9.9 percent of revenues came from interstate traffic as of the 1930s (Herring and Gross, 1936, 213). Twenty years earlier, when state regulation began to diffuse, there was considerably less interstate traffic.

State regulation was looked upon as the most appealing alternative; it was thought to be the most conservative form of regulation and the least onerous, especially compared with the municipal variety, which was often seen as radical (Garnett, 1985, 130–31).

However, there is some debate over AT&T's preference for state versus federal regulation. Garnett suggests that AT&T preferred the state variety, but Bickers (1986, 23) argues that AT&T preferred federal regulation in order to avoid nationalization. My reading is that AT&T preferred state regulation, but did not oppose federal regulation. For instance, in 1908, AT&T issued a public statement that it did not object to federal supervision, but objected to a commission (the ICC) having the power to fix rates and tariffs and to prescribe fixed forms of accounting (New York Times, 20 December 1908, 16).

State regulation would also avert the nationalization movement. Further, state regulation was aligned with the then-strong progressive movement. Bell's support of these progressive ideals would surely help the company's image. Finally, the experience of other industries with regulation proved not to be too onerous, though Bell balked somewhat at strict rate regulation. As Long (1962, 115) says about AT&T preferences for regulation: "The commissions would serve as a buffer between the Bell system and both the state legislatures and the public. As permanent bodies they would both be less amenable to the changing gusts of public opinion and more susceptible to a stable system of sympathetic contact."

It's almost as if Bell anticipated the regulatory capture that might occur under regulation—at least regulation would provide a stable environment, something then lacking in the competitive atmosphere and something that more political solutions might not allow.

During the first dozen years of the century, new and greatly empowered public utility commissions sprang up around the nation. In the few short years after Bell's turnabout in 1907 and its acceptance of regulation, Bell found itself regulated in most of the states. In 1910, federal regulation began in a small way, but it was not until 1934 that federal regulation was set in the form that it would assume for the next 50 years.

The Spread of State Regulation. Prior to 1907, eight states, mostly in the South, regulated telephones to some extent (See Table 1.1).[2] Then an outburst of state regulation commenced in 1907, and from 1907 until 1914 another 30 states and the District of Columbia began

Table 1.1

Diffusion of Telephone Regulation across the States

State	Garnet Date	NARUC, 1984 Rate Setting	NARUC, 1911 Findings
Alabama	1907	1921	Juris., No Rules
Alaska		1960	
Arizona		1912	No Juris.
Arkansas		1935	No Juris.
California	1908–11	1912	No Juris.
Colorado		1913	No Juris.
Connecticut	1908–11	1911	No Juris.
Delaware		1949	
D.C.		1913	
Florida		1913	Juris., No Rules
Georgia		1906	Juris., No Rules
Hawaii		1913	
Idaho		1913	No Response
Illinois		1913	No Juris.
Indiana	1885	1913	No Juris.
Iowa		1963	No Juris.
Kansas	1908–11	1911	No Juris.
Kentucky		1935	No Response
Louisiana	1898	1921	Juris. and Rules
Maine		1914	No Juris.
Maryland	1908–11	1910	Investigating
Massachusetts		1851	Investigating
Michigan	1908–11	1913	No Juris. (1911)
Minnesota		1915	No Juris.
Mississippi	1892	1956	No Response
Missouri		1913	No Juris.
Montana		1913	No Juris.
Nebraska	1907	1909	Juris., No Rules
Nevada	1907	1920	No Juris.
New Hampshire	1908–11	1911	No Juris. (1911)
New Jersey	1908–11	1911	Some Powers
New Mexico	1908–11	1912	
New York	1908–11	1910	Juris., No Rules
N. Carolina		1893	Juris., No Rules
N. Dakota	1908–11	1919	No Juris. (1911, No Rules)
Ohio	1908–11	1913	No Juris. (1911)
Oklahoma	1907	1917	Juris., No Rules (1911)*
Oregon	1908–11	1911	No Juris.
Pennsylvania		1913	Investigating
Rhode Island		1969	No Juris.

*Court case pending.

Table 1.1 *(continued)*

State	Garnet Date	NARUC, 1984 Rate Setting	NARUC, 1911 Findings
S. Carolina	1904	1912	Juris., No Rules
S. Dakota		1909	Juris., No Rules
Tennessee		1913	No Juris.
Texas		1976	No Juris.
Utah		1917	
Vermont	1908–11	1923	No Rules, but tariffs must be filed
Virginia		1002	Juris., No Rules
Washington	1908–11	1909	Investigating
W. Virginia		1915	No Response
Wisconsin		1907	Juris. and Rules
Wyoming		1915	No Juris.

regulating telephones. Four more stragglers (Minnesota, Utah, West Virginia, and Wyoming) regulated the telephone by the end of the decade. Thus, by 1920, 42 states and the District of Columbia regulated telephones. Sporadically over the years the remaining six continental states also regulated telephony, ending in 1976 with Texas' adoption of such regulations.[3]

The historical record on early state regulation of telephones is far from complete, but a report issued by the New York state legislature in 1910 gives us a good sense of the scope and extent of state regulations across the states.[4] The report compiled all of the statutes in the states concerning telephone regulation as of 1910 and found that 13 states had placed telephone companies under the jurisdiction of a railroad or public utility commission (sometimes also called a "public service commission"). They tended to be located in the South and West (see Table 1.2). Only Massachusetts and Vermont were so organized in the East. A few more states (15) allowed regulation of rates. Again, this set is composed mostly of the states with commission-style regulation, but Florida, Maryland, and North Dakota regulated rates to some extent without commissions, and of the commission states, only Massachusetts was not granted regulatory power over rates. Vermont's rate regulations were quite forward-looking, requiring the same rates for the same service anywhere in the state, a forerunner of statewide rate averaging that was to prove so popular. Virginia prohibited short-haul–long-haul distinctions, the much-maligned practice of the railroads prior to their regulation.

Table 1.2

Summary of Statutes Regulating Telephone Companies in 1910

	A	B	C	D	E
Alabama					
Arkansas	x	x		x	
Arizona					
California					
Colorado					
Connecticut			x	x	x
Delaware					
D.C.					
Florida		x			
Georgia	x	x			
Idaho					
Illinois					
Indiana				x	
Iowa				x	
Kansas					
Kentucky					
Louisiana	x	x		x	
Maryland		x	x	x	
Massachusetts	x		x	x	x
Michigan			x	x	
Minnesota					
Mississippi	x	x	x		
Missouri		x	x		
Montana			x		
Maine					
Nebraska	x	x			
Nevada					
New Mexico					
New Jersey					x
New York			x	x	
North Carolina	x	x			
North Dakota	x			x	x
New Hampshire					
Ohio					
Oklahoma	x	x	x	x	
Oregon					x
Pennsylvania					
Rhode Island					x
South Carolina	x	x	x		
South Dakota					
Tennessee				x	
Texas					
Utah					
Vermont	x	x	x	x	x
Virginia	x	x		x	
Washington		x	x	x	x
West Virginia					

Table 1.2 *(continued)*

	A	B	C	D	E
Wisconsin	x	x		x	
Wyoming					

Source: State of New York. 1910. *Report of the Joint Committee of the Senate and Assembly of the State of New York Appointed to Investigate Telephone and Telegraph Companies.* Appendix B. Transmitted to the Legislature March 21, 1910.

Notes:
A: Commission
    Regulation
B: Rate Regulation
C: Interconnection
    Regulation
D: Antidiscrimination
    Regulation
E: Local Citing Control

Another set of states granted broad regulatory powers, mostly ceding control of placement of utility wires, poles, and other establishments, to the localities. Of these seven states, five were in the Northeast—only North Dakota and Oregon allowed local control in the West.

Third, a number of states began to require interconnection between telephone companies and telephone and telegraph companies. Ten states had explicit interconnection requirements. Half of these were in the East and half were also commission-regulated states. Bickers (1986, 21) reports that by 1919, 34 state legislatures had passed laws requiring interconnection between competing companies.

A common form of regulation came in the form of antidiscrimination clauses. Such clauses required that service be offered to anyone who could pay for it and on a first-come, first-served basis. Nineteen states provided for such regulation—they were spread across the regions fairly evenly. Nine of the thirteen commission states had antidiscrimination regulations.

A few states had other unique regulations. California allowed abandonment of lines, Massachusetts required insulation of wiring for safety purposes, Montana and Texas had strong antimonopoly regulations, New York required underground laying of cables in large cities, Ohio and Wyoming specified regulations for poles, and Ohio and

Pennsylvania required yearly reports by the telephone companies to state agencies for other than tax purposes.

We can compute a rough index of state regulation by considering how many of the four major forms of regulation the states provided (commission control, rate regulation, interconnection, and anti-discrimination). Three states possessed all four regulatory provisions (Oklahoma, Vermont, and Washington), none of which is commonly thought of as an innovator in regulatory policy. Another eight states granted three regulatory powers to their commissions (Arkansas, Louisiana, Maryland, Massachusetts, Mississippi, South Carolina, Virginia, and Wisconsin). What is striking about these eleven regulatory leaders is the strong representation of southern states. Five of the eleven are from the old confederacy. The other six are divided among the eastern and midwestern/western states.

Another perspective on these data is to look at the regulatory laggards. Twenty-five states did not have even one such regulatory power as of 1910. Again one observes the regulatory advances of the South. Only two confederate states lacked any of these regulations, while eight states (including the District of Columbia) were to be found in the East and nine in the West. (The West is somewhat overrepresented here because of the territorial governments of Arizona and New Mexico, which were among the regulatory laggards.) The remaining six were located in the Midwest.

What accounted for this regional pattern of southern leadership? Part of it seems to be happenstance. The south engaged quite early in extensive railroad regulation. Thus, they had in place the government organizations to regulate these other utilities. But then so did the rest of the nation by 1910. The South seemed more prone to regulation of big business during the turn of the century, which may be due in part to the populist, anti–big business movements that affected those states (along with the grain Midwest) so strongly.

Further, strongly associated with southern regulation is the propensity to use it also as a means of promoting industry in that region. Much poorer than the rest of the nation, with less capital for investment, the government took on the duty of helping to build the infrastructure.[5] Viewed this way, southern regulation is less of a regulator and more of a stimulator for telephony in the South. While telephone companies were regulated in the South, regulations acted more to promote and protect than to control.

Period 4: 1914–33

In 1910, the federal government, under the jurisdiction of the Interstate Commerce Commission, tentatively began to regulate telephones. Through the 1910 Mann-Elkins Act, Congress gave the Interstate Commerce Commission the first federal powers to regulate telephones. Under that act, the ICC was granted the power to regulate rates for interstate telephone traffic. Oddly, congressional action on Mann-Elkins did not originally consider telephone matters. The thrust of the law was to grant appellate jurisdiction over railroad matters that appeared before the ICC's Commerce Court. However, on floor action, the bill was amended to include telephone, telegraph, and cable companies under ICC jurisdiction. Both Bell and independents supported the provision, though they did not make their positions public. Surely, if regulation was coming AT&T would want to affect its form (Gable, 1969, 357).

It is not clear just what impact this new ICC power had over telephone rates. In the years that the ICC regulated AT&T interstate rates, only four rates cases were brought before the commission, none of which were considered important matters. Never did the commission investigate telephone rates. Any ICC action about rates was begun only if rate complaints were made (Gable, 1969, 357). The most important regulatory actions that the ICC made during the years before telephony was brought under FCC regulation were to promulgate a uniform system of accounts and to require reports of AT&T (Herring and Gross, 1936, 64).

Lack of strong regulatory action by the ICC led the independents to bring their complaints to the Attorney General. The major concern of the independents was the AT&T policy of buying independent companies and merging them into the AT&T network. Independents brought their complaints to the Justice Department, which was more hospitable to their "social efficiency" arguments than the ICC, which was more disposed to the regulatory-equity policy regime. The Justice Department filed a suit against AT&T charging that it violated the Sherman Anti-Trust Act when it acquired a small long distance company in the Pacific Northwest. Fearing restrictive action from the federal government, AT&T Vice President N. C. Kingsbury signed an accord with Attorney General George Wickersham on December 13, 1913, commonly referred to as the Kingsbury Commitment (see Bickers, 1986,

27; Brooks, 1976, 135–36; Gable, 1969, 353; Herring and Gross, 1936, 65; Horwitz, 1986, 123; Stone, 1989, 48; Temin with Galambos, 1987, 9–11).

The main features of the commitment required AT&T to dispose of its Western Union holdings, to stop the practice of purchasing competing telephone systems, and to allow all other telephone companies toll access on its long distance system (Herring and Gross, 1936, 65). Significantly, the commitment did not prohibit AT&T from buying noncompeting exchanges, which allowed the giant to continue to expand its network and market control. Further, it defused antitrust actions against AT&T, but did not alter fundamentally the protective regulatory umbrella that AT&T had built around itself through the ICC and the state PUCs. In effect, AT&T successfully used equity arguments to fend off social efficiency attacks.

However, the Kingsbury commitment did not stop AT&T's absorption of independents. Again propelled by agitation from independents, Congress amended ICC powers with the Willis-Graham Act in 1921. That Act gave the ICC the power to oversee mergers and acquisitions of telephone companies. Willis-Graham abrogated the Kingsbury commitment, at least according to AT&T, by allowing AT&T acquisitions of competitors under ICC supervision (Horwitz, 1986, 123). As ICC supervision had been so lacking in rate cases, AT&T began a very aggressive policy of acquisition of competing exchanges. This further agitated the independents, who had many friends in Congress. Again in anticipation of stronger federal action against it, AT&T notified the independents formally that it did not intend to acquire competitors (Gable, 1969, 353). Still, federal regulation of telephone company purchases seemed far from effective. From 1921 to 1934, the years that the ICC had power to regulate AT&T's acquisitions, it approved 271 of 274 such acquisitions (Stone, 1989, 48). State PUCs also tended to approve of AT&T acquisition policy.

Relationships between the independents and AT&T settled down, as AT&T began to build a fully nationally integrated network of which the independents, who now controlled only about 20 percent of local exchanges, were to become an important part. During this period, as the threat from AT&T subsided, the independents began to adopt the equity arguments of AT&T and jettisoned their social efficiency arguments that they had used as a weapon against AT&T. While not able to grow at AT&T's expense, the independents did learn that they could prosper financially under the regulatory regime that AT&T preferred.

Thus, the experience of AT&T under federal regulation prior to the creation of the FCC suited the corporate giant well. Rarely was the company prohibited from doing what it wanted. Federal regulatory protection allowed AT&T to build the monopoly that it had always desired and sought, but that had eluded it except for a few short years in the 1880s and 1890s. In the process AT&T also adopted the government policy of equitable distribution of telephone service. AT&T would stay committed to that policy until divestiture forced it to abandon it as government policy shifted to that of social efficiency. That is the subject of the next chapter.

Summary and Theoretical Recapitulation

The early history of telephony is the tale of an industry and a government both seeking a stable solution to the telephone problem. For AT&T, the telephone problem was to acquire and maintain a stable market position, thereby ensuring some level of profitability. The government's problem was to decide how that market would relate to the general populace. As the telephone market was new and government interference in the economy was rarely practiced, the early period was noted as one of shifting positions, arrangements, and policies among the active participants.

Over time, pressure on government mounted, demanding that it control the distribution and operation of telephone service. That pressure shifted government policy away from the traditional laissez-faire doctrine to one of regulation. Though elements in the nation proposed nationalization, and the government flirted with the idea, it never took hold in any substantial form. Similarly, AT&T began to see the advantages of regulation. Not only did regulation defuse nationalization sentiment, but it provided more stability than laissez-faire, and it could be used to counter antitrust, the major policy weapon that AT&T's competitors possessed. Further, regulation opened the door to amicable relations between the government and AT&T. While regulation did have strings attached, and while periods of friction did develop between AT&T and the government, regulation's intent was never to do harm to the company, but merely to ensure its profitable operation toward the public interest. Thus, after much fumbling, government at all levels and AT&T, along with the independents, created a stable regulatory regime.

However, the seeds of contradiction were planted in government policy at the federal level. It never decided definitively the role of antitrust toward telephony and AT&T. Repositing antitrust protection in the Antitrust Division of the Department of Justice and regulation in the Federal Communications Commission set the basis for future conflict over jurisdiction and proper policy goals as applied to telephony. Time and again, AT&T would fend off antitrust threats, and usually would do so successfully—that is, until the threats of the late 1970s and 1980s. These culminated in divestiture—the triumph of antitrust over regulation and of social efficiency over equity. That is the story for the next chapter.

The present chapter has developed a number of themes that will be important in building our theory of influence in the public policy process. In particular, we have examined the two competing policy directions, economic efficiency and equity, that would later shape state responses to divestiture. We saw the connection between antitrust and economic efficiency and that between regulation and equity-universal service, and how two other policy courses, laissez-faire and nationalization, were closed off from public consideration and debate.

This chapter also revealed the utility of the multiple interest perspective. Originally, only AT&T and the federal government were active participants in telecommunications. Later other interests, the independent telephone companies, consumers, and business users, were added into the equation. In the next chapter, we will examine how state politicians and bureaucrats became participants in the policy subsystem, along with public interest groups, rounding out the contours of the policy subsystem as divestiture approached. Full development of the theory, the conditional impact of resources on policy making, will come in later chapters.

Notes

1. Some proponents of nationalization argue that it can actually work more efficiently than the market. Waste due to competitive duplication is eliminated. Underpinning these theories of nationalization are ideas that the market might not exist in some economic realms—rather, natural monopolies do. However, in the United States, the corrective to the natural monopoly problem has been regulation, highlighting the power of market theory in the American political culture.

2. It is difficult from the historical record to determine definitively when states began regulation of the telephones and the nature of that regulation. For

instance, the 1984 National Association of Regulatory Utility Commissioners (NARUC) report on carriers says that Massachusetts began regulation of telephone rates in 1851, which is impossible, as telephones were only invented in 1876. (See NARUC, 1977–1985a, 437.) Further, Holmes states in an 1890 essay: "the telephone business [is] not yet under the supervision of commissioners, but selectmen and mayors and aldermen may establish reasonable regulations" (1890, 423). What we do know is that the early Bell companies were incorporated in Massachusetts, and therefore came under the general corporation regulations noted above. The 1911 NARUC study found Massachusetts was then only investigating whether or not to regulate telephones (see NARUC, 1911, 211–18.) However, a 1910 New York state compilation of statutes relating to telephones and telegraphs found that Massachusetts regulated the telephones under the authority of the Highway Commission, but that authority was not granted rate-making power, and much local control still prevailed in the state at that time. (See State of New York, 1910, 113–25.)

3. The six comprise quite a varied lot: Arkansas, 1935; Delaware, 1949; Iowa, 1963; Kentucky, 1935; Rhode Island, 1969; Texas, 1976.

4. The succeeding paragraphs are based on that report (State of New York, 1910). Another valuable source is the National Civic Federation (1913). The federation report compiled all statutes as of 1913 concerning regulation of utilities by commission. It is well indexed and cross-referenced.

5. There is little about promotion of telephony, but Du Boff (1984) does a good job describing southern promotion of the telegraph. As telegraphy and telephony are so closely intertwined during the era, it is quite likely that programs similar to those for telegraphy were used to promote telephony. Mostly, they tended to be grants of rights-of-way arrangements with railroads, sometimes subscribing to stock issuances. (See Du Boff, 1984, 60–64; also relevant are Lipartito, 1988 and 1989.)

2

The Regulatory Regime from the Federal Communications Act to Divestiture, 1934–84

Introduction

In 1934, AT&T came under the regulatory supervision of the newly created Federal Communications Commission (FCC). For the next 50 years a stable, but sometimes tense, relationship developed between the regulator and the telephone company. Tension-producing currents that occasionally surfaced included AT&T's image as an unbridled monopoly and the contradiction in government policy between social efficiency versus equity. As long as AT&T was viewed as monopolistic, the antitrust arguments of the efficiency advocates could be energized and activated. The problem for AT&T and the regulators was to determine AT&T's legitimate scope as a monopoly—its boundary. Outside of that boundary, the monopoly was forbidden entry. If AT&T was to be protected from the antitrust regime at the Department of Justice (DOJ), clear lines would have to be demarcated indicating where AT&T could act as a responsible regulated monopoly—a monopoly that provided the nation with valued telecommunications services based on a public policy of equitable distribution to and treatment of customers. By deciding the limits of the monopoly and regulation, the government could balance its contradictory efficiency and equity policies. Thus, the provision of telephone service came under a policy regime of monopoly, regulation, and equity. Outside of that area, antitrust would govern.

The FCC and AT&T:
The Tension between Equity and Efficiency

When the FCC was created, it assumed the powers and duties of the old Federal Radio Commission and the regulatory powers that the Interstate Commerce Commission (ICC) had concerning telephone, telegraph, and cable. The FCC was not invested with new powers. Rather it was viewed as an administrative reorganization that could more effectively regulate the growing electronic communications industry (Stone, 1989, 57–8). However, the politics of the New Deal also opened the possibility that the FCC would regulate AT&T more vigorously than the ICC, which had been more concerned with railroad regulation and which had never been a very ardent regulator. By combining all telecommunications regulation within one agency, it was hoped that the federal government could develop expertise in telecommunications engineering and accounting that would allow it to watch more keenly the actions and behaviors of telecommunications providers.

Early on, AT&T's relationship with the FCC deteriorated in ways that had never happened with the ICC. The specter of its monopolistic intentions and the anti–big business rhetoric and policy of the New Deal created a climate rife with antagonism between the regulator and the regulated. In effect, as a young agency the FCC was trying to develop a balance between the competing claims of equity and efficiency, of regulation and antitrust.

The early FCC attack on AT&T was based on a theory of monopoly and predatory pricing, which the DOJ would revive in the suit leading to divestiture. The theory of predation argues that when a firm has a monopoly in one market but is competitive in another, it will engage in predatory price wars in the competitive market, supported by monopolistic pricing behavior in the monopoly market. In effect, in the competitive market, the monopoly will drive prices below costs to force its competitors out of the market. The firm can afford to do this by raising prices in its monopoly market well above costs. These excess profits are then used to subsidize the predatory pricing policies in the competitive market. After defeating its competitors, the monopoly can extend its control into the once competitive market, but now as a monopoly.[1]

While regulators at the time did not want to undo the equity regime in the provision of telephone service, they did want to prevent AT&T from using its monopoly power there to control other markets. Thus,

AT&T's vertically integrated structure came under attack for the first of many times. AT&T's ownership of Western Electric, its manufacturing arm, came under the most criticism.

Western Electric was the largest manufacturer of telephone equipment in the United States, producing equipment from telephones to switching stations to telephone lines. Its sole customer was AT&T. Fears were that Western overcharged AT&T, which then passed these overcharges onto customers through inflation of the rate base. Thus, AT&T was able to secure excess profits—profits that were more than "just and reasonable," as regulatory statutes guarantee.

Under a congressional mandate to investigate all aspects of the telephone industry, the FCC began its inquiry in 1935, concluding its effort in 1938 after expending nearly $2,000,000 of taxpayer money and $1,500,000 of AT&T money (huge sums for that day), plus employing over 300 staff researchers (Brooks, 1976, 196–98). The investigation produced 77 volumes, totaling 8,500 pages of scathing criticism of AT&T (Federal Communications Commission, 1938; Stone, 1989, 62).[2] The investigation's leader, Commissioner Paul Walker, offered rather radical proposals, not subscribed to by the other FCC commissioners, which included the direct federal regulation of Western Electric's prices and which required AT&T to purchase equipment through competitive bidding (Anonymous, 1939; Brooks, 1976, 198; Stone, 1989, 61–66). Congressional support for AT&T, less critical attitudes of the other FCC commissioners, and the looming specter of world war quieted the situation, but the issue of AT&T's relationship with Western Electric would echo through the postwar period.

Thus, the policy problems associated with telephone service began to crystallize in the 1930s. Service integration of the network (i.e., the provision of end-to-end customer service), including local and long distance, was viewed positively because it promoted the highly valued equity policy, by now known as *universal service*. Further, by viewing the creation of the network as desirable because of its natural monopoly character, efficiency arguments were defused. In a state of natural monopoly, efficiency is promoted through integration and suppression of wasteful competition. However, the company's vertical integration was viewed as a threat to other truly competitive markets. Thus the possibility (and perhaps need) to interpose antitrust against AT&T. However, from the 1930s until the mid-1950s, the states would be the more important regulatory arena, and equity would be the dominant policy regime.

State Regulation, 1934–84

State regulation of AT&T and the independents was based on promotion of universal service and equity. Value-based pricing was the regulatory theory implemented in all of the states. Such pricing led to rate averaging and cross-subsidization of some customer classes by others. In all, AT&T's relations with the states were congenial, though lurking in the shadows was the threat of federal preemption. By the time of divestiture, the FCC, through preemption theory, had come to dominate the regulation of AT&T, leaving the states with few responsibilities, except for setting local rate levels and structures, and determining acceptable levels of service. As divestiture neared, and the FCC and DOJ came to be seen as threats to AT&T's integrated service network, the state regulators naturally allied themselves with the telephone company.

The Structure of Rates in the States

Over time, AT&T and the independent telephone companies found allies among the state regulators—the various state public utility commissions (PUCs). This alliance developed because AT&T supported a pricing structure that offered political benefits to the PUCs. Primarily, AT&T supported value-based pricing and its implementation through rate averaging, which promoted the universal service goal. The PUCs built strong public support, especially in rural areas and among consumers, by promoting universal service. Not only was the equity argument attractive to these groups, who might otherwise be unable to afford telephone service, but universal service policies helped meet the huge demand among consumers for telephone service.

By the 1960s and 1970s, the states had successfully completed the movement toward universal service. By 1960 nearly 80 percent of households had telephone service; in the 1980s the percentage topped 90 percent. In the years afterward attempts were made by state regulators to preserve and protect their universal-service accomplishment. They felt that maintenance of the existing relationship granting AT&T a regulated monopoly, the absence of competition, and the adherence to an equity policy regime were necessary to ensure the survival of universal service.

The conservatism of the state regulators about universal service and their fears concerning its vulnerability were grounded in experience. During the 1920–40 period, rural telephony declined after many years of strong growth. "One million fewer American farms had telephones in 1940 than did in 1920. In 1940, 25 percent of all farms had telephones; 39 percent did in 1920" (Fischer, 1987, 295). Fischer, the major scholar in this field, suggests that substitution effects from automobiles and the disinterest of major telephone companies in rural telephony explain the decline. As he further states, "When the telephone was a natural monopoly, farmers were largely unserved. When competition was rife, they had more telephones than did urbanites. When local monopoly was restored, farmers fell behind. And when effective government intervention developed in the 1940s, the city–country gap narrowed rapidly" (Fischer, 1987, 312).

That effective government policy was the implementation of universal service and value-based pricing under regulatory oversight. The PUCs were to ensure that AT&T and the independents extended service to all. To effectuate this policy, a complex pricing scheme was developed in which a number of cross-subsidies were created. Within the states, businesses were charged more for service than were consumers (residents), and urban areas were assessed somewhat higher than rural and small town areas. However, the cross-subsidy most appealing to local interests was the one from long distance users to the local operating companies. Through this policy, telephone revenues were redistributed from the federal level to the states. This helped suppress local rates and helped spur the extension of the state universal-service mission.

Separations

Crucial to the effectuation of universal service was the cross-subsidization of local service by long distance.[3] To understand why and how this cross-subsidization policy was implemented requires distinguishing between two theories of pricing of long distance service—board-to-board versus station-to-station. Board-to-board communication links the local telephone exchange with the toll network, the long distance lines. Station-to-station communication links the call from the telephone (the station) to the other telephone. In the board-to-board call, only the component of the call traveling from one board to the other is assigned to long distance; the part of the call that connects the station (e.g., the home telephone) to the board is considered purely local. Station-to-station considers even the part of a long distance call that connects the station to the board as partially long distance. In effect, station-to-station theory assigns part of the operation of the local loop to long distance operations. Undergirding this theory was the idea that since long distance had to use the local loop to complete a call, long distance should pay for the maintenance and development of the local network. It was argued that long distance would not be possible without the local network.[4] By the end of the Second World War, station to-station emerged as the option that policy makers preferred. Their problem, however, was how to separate long distance from local costs over the station-to-board connection.

Motivating the adoption of station-to-station instead of board-to-board were (1) the increase in long distance calling with the Second World War, and (2) the resultant increase in AT&T's profits. Federal regulators sought a way to reduce AT&T's profits without lowering the price of long distance calls. What policy makers wanted to avoid was increased utilization of long lines, which they wanted to preserve for the war effort. By assigning part of the revenue from a long distance call to the local network, they could allocate some of the profits from long distance to the local network, thus reducing AT&T's profits and helping universal service in the states.

Station-to-station theory had a beauty to those interested in promoting universal service. By requiring AT&T Long Lines, the company's long distance unit, to add to its operating costs part of the local loop, AT&T's profits fell. Simultaneously, the local operating companies could deduct those parts now being paid for by AT&T. The resultant reductions in local operating costs could then be passed on to the local subscriber in the form of lower rates, thereby encouraging universal service.

By 1947 AT&T and the FCC had developed a satisfactory separations procedure to determine what part of the local system could reasonably be charged to long distance. The theory developed was based on a concept of "subscriber line use" (SLU) that was based on relative use of the local plant by long distance and local calls. While this costing policy affected local rates, the FCC did not initially intend that long distance would "cross-subsidize" local operations.

By the end of World War II, it became apparent that *intra*state long distance calls were becoming comparatively more expensive than *inter-state* long distance. Local regulators felt that this toll gap could be narrowed by increasing the separations charges allocated against long distance. While the FCC initially resisted such a policy, local regulators had powerful friends in Congress, and in 1950, fearing congressional action, the FCC capitulated to congressional desires and began renegotiating separations procedures with AT&T. Beginning in 1950, the transfer of money from long distance to local began to supersede the estimated SLU. By 1980, the SLU was estimated at about 7 percent, but the size of the transfer from long distance to local operations stood at about 25 percent.

As board-to-board costs were dropping, however, the costs of providing long distance were not increasing, but actually *decreasing*. This enabled the increased subsidy to local operations without increasing the price of long distance calls. Yet, this also set in place a price–cost gap that business would recognize and would lead in part to divestiture.

Business could net a handsome profit and eat into AT&T's long distance market if vendors of telephone service could avoid the separations charges that AT&T paid, and such avoidance was most likely if these other vendors could avoid using the public network, that is, by-pass the public network. They could do this by offering private line communications to large users. The costs of operating these private line systems would not include charges to the public network—the separations charges. Some of these savings could be passed on to the new customers, allowing new vendors to attract customers while still retaining substantial profits. This was in part the economic strategy of Microwave Communications, Inc. (MCI), which would become crucial to the full divestiture of AT&T. By letting such operations into the market, the FCC would begin to undermine the monopoly network of AT&T, just as it had earlier attacked the vertical structure of the network. By the late 1970s, AT&T was being attacked on both fronts.

Federal Preemption and the Theory of Local Effects

While the FCC, AT&T, and the local regulators began to develop a costing accord through separations that seemed to benefit all, tension between the federal and state regulators slowly began to build. Incrementally, the federals began to preempt local regulatory power under the theory of local effects.

Initially state regulators found themselves in a strong position when the Supreme Court issued its *Smith* v. *Illinois Bell* decision in 1930. A decision of varied and far-reaching consequence, it enabled state regulators to inspect Western Electric's charges to the local telephone companies, thereby allowing the state regulators access to important information concerning the costs of operating the system. As Western Electric was the sole provider of equipment to AT&T and its local subsidiaries, regulators required such information to ensure that Western Electric was not overcharging the local operating companies for equipment and plant. Coming to such conclusions was difficult, as no competitive market for telephone goods existed. Yet, access to information about Western's operations and costs were crucial to local regulation if it was even to begin to make a reasonable stab at rate regulation. Further, access on the part of all state PUCs and the FCC to the same information ensured a comparability across the states and prevented Western from treating states discriminately (Stone, 1989, 76).

The theory of local effects was used successfully by the FCC to supersede state regulation and require state compliance with federal standards, practices, and policy. Beginning with the New Deal, the FCC and the federal courts began to exert authority over actions by state regulators under power derived from a liberal interpretation of the Commerce Clause, from which federal regulatory power derives. Basically, as the decisions of local regulators may affect interstate commerce and the quality of the integrated telephone network under federal regulation, the FCC and the courts began to preempt local decisions (Stone, 1989, 15).

This became one element of conflict between state and federal regulators as divestiture neared. Not only were the FCC and other federal agencies moving toward an antitrust standard, while the states preferred the utility regulation policy, but the federal regulators, through their preemptive powers, began to force the states away from the utility regulatory regime (with its emphasis on equity), toward more competitive local policies (with their emphasis on efficiency).

Attacking the AT&T Regulated Monopoly

After the Second World War, AT&T's regulated monopoly was confronted with a series of attacks on both its vertical and integrated network structure. In almost all cases, the attacks centered on where the monopoly's boundaries should be placed. Outside the boundary, AT&T would be prohibited entry. Within those lines, AT&T's structure would remain intact. Only with divestiture was it decided to transport AT&T itself outside of the protections of regulated monopolization, even though its offshoots, the divested "Baby Bells," would retain regulation and control of local communications. Also, across the years, distinguishing between the vertical and integrated network components of the system became intertwined, and decisions to allow competition with vertical aspects of system structure would begin to affect network integration. The story of AT&T's road to divestiture has been well told in numerous places (Bickers, 1986, 32–47; Coll, 1986; Derthick and Quirk, 1985, 177–202; Henck and Strassburg, 1988; Horwitz, 1986; Kahaner, 1986; Kraus and Duerig, 1988; Stone, 1989; Temin with Galambos, 1987; von Auw, 1983). Hence, I will not repeat it here in detail. However, to understand the policy reactions of the states, my major concern, requires filling in the historical context from which those policies emanated. Thus, I present a brief discussion of the major events and themes along the road to divestiture.

Restricting the Monopoly: The 1949 Western Electric Case

In 1949, the Department of Justice picked up where the FCC had left off a decade earlier. That year, DOJ began an antitrust suit against AT&T with the aim of divesting Western Electric from the corporate giant. The case commenced during one of the most vigorous periods of antitrust action by the federal government, the Truman administration of the late 1940s (Stone, 1989, 69).

After years of relative inaction, AT&T and DOJ entered into their first modern consent agreement in 1956,[5] one that would set a pattern for later relations between the two, the precedent for which was the Kingsbury commitment of 40 years earlier (see chapter 1). The Consent Decree provided that (1) Western Electric would have to sell its subsidiary Westrex, the motion-picture sound equipment manufacturer (pulling out of nontelephony had already begun at Western Electric and AT&T more generally); (2) AT&T would not enter unregulated markets, except for special work for the federal government[6]; (3) Western electric would be required to maintain cost accounting methods that would enable regulators to better determine the appropriate price for the equipment that it sold to AT&T; and (4) AT&T would enter into liberal patent licensing agreements with other companies, a policy already beginning at AT&T (Stone, 1989, 77–79).

In coming to the agreement AT&T preserved its vertical structure, but at a cost: AT&T would be prohibited from entering markets that were unregulated and unrelated to its primary telephone service mission. By accepting this restriction, AT&T hoped to protect itself from antitrust actions by setting up firm boundaries between its regulated structure and competitive, unregulated markets, thereby discrediting any future attempts to suggest that AT&T was engaging in anticompetitive practices.

As the company would learn, those arguments would fall on deaf ears and any actions of its own to avoid the appearance of anticompetitive practices would fall on blind eyes. AT&T's history as an aggressive monopolizer during the turn of the century, its spirited protection and accumulation of patents, its excursions into nontelephone industries (such as computers, radio, television, and motion pictures), Bell Laboratories' inventions outside of telephony, and the sheer size of the company all created suspicions about AT&T's true intentions and ability to act as a responsible corporation, even under regulation.

The 1956 Consent Decree set the basis for the next 25 years of regulation of telephones in the United States. (The Modified Final Judgment of 1982, which implemented divestiture, was a modification of the 1956 Consent Decree.) The government believed that AT&T's relationship with its subsidiary Western Electric led to higher costs for equipment and higher profits for AT&T than if AT&T were forced to enter into competitive bidding for equipment. AT&T felt otherwise— that savings accrued from doing business with one firm intimately knowledgeable about AT&T operations. Further, savings increased by ensuring that customized equipment would be provided by a company with an understanding of standardization requirements of the network. These integrity-of-the-network arguments would be a major basis of AT&T's defense against future assaults.

Competition in Equipment and the Radio Spectrum

With AT&T's monopoly now firmly in place, but also bounded, competitors began to chip away at AT&T's market, arguing that the company was unable and unwilling to meet new demands for new types of services and products. In fact, economic theory then and now argues that monopoly and regulation retard innovation and new product and service development. Regulation of common carriers was based on the idea that common carriers and other public utilities would be granted a monopoly only if they were willing and able to provide all services that were demanded. If a new demand arose that did not undermine the integrity of the network and AT&T was neither offering that service nor likely to, another vender could do so. And if that new demand did not affect the integrity of the network—if it was considered outside of AT&T's traditional and regulated purview—other firms, regulated or unregulated, could offer the service. This occurred on two fronts, the first concerning equipment, the second concerning allocation of the radio spectrum.

Equipment Interconnections

Hush-a-Phone

The *Hush-a-Phone* decision in 1956 opened the door to interconnection of customer premise equipment to the telephone network (Stone, 1989, 121–25; Horwitz, 1986, 135–37). *Hush-a-Phone* was an acoustical cup that attached to the telephone receiver to promote privacy of conversations, especially in crowded conditions. As the device did not require any electrical components, it did not affect system safety. However, according to AT&T engineers, transmission quality was affected significantly and cupping the hand over the receiver was found to be more effective.

The case traveled from the FCC to the Court of Appeals, District of Columbia Circuit, where, according to Stone, for the first time in a telecommunications case a federal court made a decision on the substance of a case, not merely on matters of fact and law. In effect, Stone argues, the Court of Appeals in deciding for *Hush-a-Phone* set a precedent for judicial activism that would continue through to divestiture (Stone, 1989, 123).

In its decision the Court of Appeals set a new standard with potentially far-reaching consequences by stating that interconnection of customer premise equipment could not be prohibited if the device does not harm the system physically. In response, AT&T developed new interconnection standards, distinguishing between harmful and harmless devices. Those without electrical components tended to be viewed as harmless; all electrically based interconnecting devices, however, were viewed by AT&T as potentially harmful.

Carterfone

While *Hush-a-Phone* opened the way for interconnection of equipment to the network, the decision was relatively narrow, and the market for *Hush-a-Phones* was relatively small. However, the *Carterfone* decision in 1968 had greater market implications.

Carterfone was essentially a device that connected a two-way mobile radio to a telephone, which allowed the radio operator to connect into the telephone network. Among the businesses that found the device so appealing were oil companies, which used it especially for off-shore oil installation communications, and shipping firms, for ship-to-shore communications (Bickers, 1986, 36–37; Horwitz, 1986, 136; Stone, 1989, 140–42, 146–52).

Demand for the device was great and neither AT&T nor the independent telephone companies were offering a similar service. Further, federal regulators felt that users could best develop the device to meet their own individual needs, thereby offering a rationale to exclude AT&T from providing such services and allowing a greater range of interconnections to the systems than the earlier *Hush-a-Phone* decision permitted. The FCC decided that as long as the device does not harm the system and a demand for it exists, such interconnection should be allowed. Allowing *Carterfone* opened the door to the computer interconnections decisions that would prove so damaging to the boundary that the 1956 Consent Decree erected.

Computers

While the *Hush-a-Phone* and *Carterfone* decisions allowed attachment of nonharmful devices to the telephone network, thereby ending AT&T's role as total end-to-end service provider, the growing similarity between computers and communications technologies served to undermine the 1956 Consent Decree's dictum to restrain AT&T from entering computer markets. Technological development began to render the computer–communication boundary obsolete.

In two decisions, *Computer I* and *Computer II*, issued in 1971 and 1976, the FCC tried to grapple with the issues that computer–

communicatioŋs technologies posed. In distinguishing between computers and communications technologies, the FCC tried to hold on to a distinction between *transmitting messages* (communicating) and *processing information* (computing). In *Computer I*, it held that regulated communications common carriers should not be able to enter data-processing markets, relying on a standard of the *primary* service offered to define what was computing and what was communicating. However, the FCC opened a can of worms with its *hybrid* category, where information was both processed and transmitted (Stone, 1989, 205–16, 260–72).

With *Computer II* the FCC began to notice that "hybrid" services were beginning to comprise larger and larger markets. Again, the FCC tried to distinguish between services, now termed *basic transmission* and *enhanced services*. Basic transmission applied only to common carriers offering the movement of information. However, enhanced service added computer processing to information communicated across the telecommunications networks. Common carriers were to be prohibited from directly offering enhanced services except through fully separated subsidiaries, from which regulators could easily distinguish regulated services and earnings from the enhanced services and their earnings. Through this decision the FCC opened the door through which AT&T could enter computing, but with the 1956 Consent Decree still in force the FCC and AT&T would have to seek legal or legislative judgment to allow AT&T's entry into these unregulated markets. Thus, *Computer II* tore down the boundary that the 1956 Consent Decree had erected in principle, but not in fact.[7]

At least in equipment, between the *Hush-a-Phone* and *Computer II* decisions the FCC had moved from the standards of the regulatory regime to those of antitrust. AT&T, however, found itself in a precarious situation. While still restricted by the regulatory regime, it now faced competitors who chipped away at its market control, which AT&T clearly wanted to protect. Decisions regarding spectrum allocation and service competition would knock down the regulatory regime in those markets, as well, furthering AT&T's discomfort.

Spectrum Allocation and Service Competition

Just as the equipment interconnection decisions were leading down the path of liberalization and ease of entry, decisions regarding the radio spectrum were also lowering barriers to entry in AT&T's once regulatory-protected markets. This became a second front where AT&T's boundary was eroded and where competition, antitrust, and efficiency arguments began to overthrow the regulatory regime of equity, value-based pricing, cost-averaging, and universal service.

The Case of Above 890Mc

In the 1940s and 1950s, in a series of decisions relating to the development of the television, the FCC decided that allocation of the microwave spectrum should be considered a scarce resource. At the time, two forms of long distance communication existed, microwave and coaxial cable. Coaxial seemed to be the more well developed, but by the 1960s new technologies, including space satellites, began to open the door to more advanced microwave communications (Horwitz, 1986, 133–35; Bickers, 1986, 31–32; Stone, 1989, 128–34).

Demand for microwave communications was great; large business users could develop private lines, thereby not only connecting far-flung points of operation, but bypassing the traditional network and evading rate-averaging payments. Thus, the costs of communication could be reduced to these large users, and communications systems developed that were tailored to their particular needs.

As to be expected, AT&T objected to the development of private lines over the microwave spectrum. For one thing, AT&T felt that it could offer such services, and perhaps more crucially, it felt that opening private line entry would undermine the universal-service principal. Those who would opt for private lines were heavy users of the long distance network. Long distance was providing a large subsidy to local and residential customers, thereby keeping those rates down and allowing the achievement of universal service. Development of private line systems would in effect skim off the most profitable elements of the telephone system from the network. Simultaneously, costs for operating the telephone network would not decline appreciably. To recoup the lost revenues, rates would have to be increased, which might threaten universal service. These same arguments were made in the case leading to divestiture, and the problem of securing universal service under competition is the major policy problem of the states in the postdivestiture era.

From another perspective, this debate clearly reveals the class-based differences between efficiency-competition policies and equity-universal service ones. The universal service–regulatory regime with its emphasis on equity looks to the aggregate social good of providing all with a certain service or product. Under the regulatory regime, if capture has not set in, transfers of wealth from rich to poor may be realized. However, under the antitrust regime, with its promotion of competition and aggregate social efficiency, the transfer of wealth from rich to poor is denied. Instead the proper workings of the market become the objects of policy. Whereas regulation is concerned with equitable distribution, antitrust is concerned with fair competition. Large users of telecommunications have a natural incentive to alter the system from regulation to antitrust—they are able to retain the wealth that regulation appropriated. Thus, the debate between antitrust and regulation in telecommunications can be seen in class terms.

In *Above 890Mc* in 1959 the FCC allowed specialized communications services to develop outside of the traditional network. Reversing earlier policy, the FCC now determined that there was no shortage of microwave frequencies and also projected that demand for such services would be small; therefore, little economic harm would come to the system. Further, the FCC felt that private point-to-point communications constituted a new type of service that did not compete with traditional telephone services. Through this logic, the FCC hoped to induce new product and service development in telecommunications through competition, which it felt to be a superior road to innovation than regulated monopoly, while at the same time protecting the integrated telephone network. The distinction between new services and traditional ones thus becomes crucial. Later MCI would use those same arguments against AT&T.

TELPAK

Realizing the impact of *Above 890Mc* on its operations, AT&T in 1960 asked the FCC for permission to offer TELPAK. TELPAK was designed to meet the needs of business users for specialized communications capability that the *Above 890Mc* proceedings revealed (Stone, 1989, 134–40; Temin with Galambos, 1987, 28–40).

AT&T Long Lines rates were nationally uniform. They did not discriminate between high and low cost routes, but practiced nationwide rate averaging. However, this rate system was threatened by *Above 890Mc*; AT&T felt that competitors would begin to provide service in the low-cost routes, which would be less expensive than the averaged AT&T rate.

TELPAK was an answer to these concerns. TELPAK offered AT&T's own private line service for the same costs to private users that they would incur by constructing their own systems. This led to cuts in AT&T rates of from one-half to seven-eighths on these routes (Temin with Galambos, 1987, 32). Such severe cuts led to suspicions concerning AT&T's intentions and motives—that AT&T might be engaged in predatory pricing. FCC and AT&T disputed the costing of TELPAK services; the FCC could not believe such reductions were feasible and not predatory. However, few then understood the huge differences between competitive and regulatory prices. In the process, the FCC denied the TELPAK offerings. As in *Above 890Mc*, the FCC seemed to want to promote competition. TELPAK, it feared, would hand most of the microwave private line market to AT&T. This decision also paved the way for the MCI assault on AT&T beginning in the mid-1960s.

MCI's Challenges

In 1963 MCI requested permission to offer private line microwave communication between Chicago and St. Louis. The service MCI wished to offer would include a mix of voice and data transmission in bundles and packages that AT&T did not then offer. MCI's intention was to offer private line communication to small businesses, which had been prohibitively expensive for them until MCI's proposal. They intended to make such service affordable by allowing several small businesses to share the lines. However, MCI did not then suggest that its offerings would be connected to the Bell network, nor would MCI provide interconnection between its subscribers and MCI. Further, MCI made no claims to offer transmission of the same quality as AT&T's services. After great delay, probably induced by all parties involved, the FCC ruled that MCI's proposal did not compete with AT&T, but that it offered a new service to a small market then unserved by AT&T.

In response to the FCC's ruling, the Commission was flooded with requests to offer services both similar to and different from that granted by MCI (Stone, 1989, 170). Seeing that its MCI decision would not be limited to the Chicago–St. Louis trunk, the FCC began its

Special Common Carrier Investigation (SCC) in 1970. That investigation suggested that all Special Common Carriers, as MCI and similar applicants now came to be known, should be allowed free entry into the market. The report suggested that telecommunications' demand for microwave communications and special services would expand greatly. Granting the SCCs market entry would not compete with AT&T because they represented market expansion, not the skimming of profitable elements of existing markets, or so the FCC report argued.

Further, the great growth in volume of voice transmissions that AT&T and the other common carriers were facing would mean that they would probably be unable to meet the demand for SCC services. Too much growth was occurring in the industry for AT&T to handle alone and under traditional regulatory mechanisms. The FCC envisioned expansion principally of two kinds of services undelivered by AT&T—data transmission, both local and intercity, and dedicated private line, point-to-point transmission, such as MCI's (Stone, 1989, 171–75; Temin with Galambos, 1987, 51–53).

In later requests, MCI filed to increase the number of cities that it could serve and also to be allowed to interconnect with the Bell system. The FCC granted both types of requests, but developing a rate tariff to allow MCI interconnection with AT&T proved difficult as MCI and AT&T based their costs on different standards. The difficulty of negotiations between MCI and AT&T on these and other matters, plus MCI's poor financial position, led the upstart company in 1974 to file a private antitrust action against AT&T.

The case, *MCI v. AT&T,* was brought to jury trial, but not until 1980, when MCI won a stunning victory and an antitrust award of $1.8 billion.[8] Jolted by the magnitude of the defeat, AT&T appealed the case and won the right of appeal and a new jury trial, which began in 1985. This time the award was reduced to $37.8 million (trebled to $113.3 million). However, by this time, AT&T had already been divested, fundamentally altering the relationship between AT&T and the SCCs, and all other outstanding MCI antitrust suits against AT&T had already been settled (Coll, 1986, 27–35; Henck and Strassburg, 1988, 190–203; Kahaner, 1986, 97–99, 167–70; Stone, 1989, 248–53; Temin with Galambos, 1987, 107–8, 207–8).

MCI's poor financial posture in 1974 lead it to try to compete with AT&T directly, hoping for FCC protection. Thus, MCI requested to be allowed to offer its EXECUNET services in 1974. An EXECUNET customer would gain access to the MCI intercity network by calling a local MCI telephone number, from which the customer could then connect to any telephone in a city that MCI served. EXECUNET was essentially the same as AT&T's WATS or MTS service (Stone, 1989, 241–42, 253). However, unlike rate-averaged MTS, EXECUNET, by focusing on high-density/low-cost routes, could be priced well below MTS. Naturally, AT&T objected, arguing that EXECUNET was nothing more than traditional long distance but offered by an SCC. If implemented, AT&T argued, the separations process and revenues to the local operating companies would be jeopardized. In 1975, the FCC issued a decision agreeing with AT&T, thereby cancelling EX-ECUNET. In response, MCI filed an appeal in the Court of Appeals for the District of Columbia (Stone, 1989, 255–58; Temin with Galambos, 1987, 134–40).

In a decision affirming MCI's right to offer EXECUNET, Judge J. Skelly Wright distinguished between services and facilities, arguing that while duplications of *facilities* were prohibited because of their potential waste, duplication of *services* was not (Stone, 1989, 256–58; Temin with Galambos, 1987, 134–45).[9] Because of the EXECUNET decision allowing MCI to offer service outside of the separations process, its competitive position and earnings improved markedly (Kahaner, 1986, 141–47).[10]

The EXECUNET decision had grave consequences for the protective boundary that AT&T and the Department of Justice erected with the Consent Decree in 1956. Competitors now seemed able to enter AT&T's protected markets, but AT&T felt restraints from DOJ and the FCC from voyaging outside of that market.

The United States versus *AT&T*

In 1974, the Department of Justice entered the arena by bringing antitrust action against AT&T. The legion of attacks against AT&T now loomed large. The FCC was handing down decisions that eroded AT&T's boundary through the customer premise, computer, and SCC decisions. MCI was challenging AT&T in the courts. Now, DOJ was bringing a major suit against AT&T.

The theory behind the DOJ suit was that AT&T engaged in monopolistic, anticompetitive practices. Among the specific types of allegations charged against AT&T was that it practiced predation, created entry barriers, and restricted interconnection (Evans, 1983; MacAvoy and Robinson, 1983, 1985). Specifically, DOJ charged that Western Electric's relationship with AT&T stifled competition among equipment manufacturers and suppliers: that AT&T's actions regarding interconnection of the SCCs and customer premise equipment amounted to obstructionism. The legal remedy that DOJ sought was the divestiture from AT&T of Western Electric and some of the local operating companies.

AT&T Goes to Congress

In 1976 AT&T began a campaign in Congress for legislation that would set the industry back to the old days of regulated and protected monopoly, killing the trend toward competition.[11] AT&T has strong support among the independent telephone companies, through their umbrella organization, the United States Independent Telephone Association (USITA); the industry's unionized work force, the Communication Workers of America (CWA); and many of the state PUCs, under their own organization, the National Association of Regulatory Utility Commissioners (NARUC). Then-president of AT&T John de Butts began a strategy reminiscent of Theodore Vail's in 1907—de Butts aimed to educate the public on the merits of the regulated industry structure, pointing out the efficiency, cost, and quality of the integrated network. Common to public folklore since the maturation of the network was that the American telephone system was the best in the world (Wall Street Journal, 22 November 1974, 18).

Galvanizing public opinion was the only strategy open to AT&T. Other strong, pro-competitive interests opposed AT&T, including the SCCs and the computer industry. The SCCs, especially MCI, were in a good public position, appearing as small companies challenging the AT&T behemoth. Natural support for the underdog was one obstacle to AT&T's mobilization of public support. Further, the administration had taken a pro-competitive posture. Not only had the FCC begun the process of allowing competition into the industry, the DOJ was doing likewise with its antitrust suit, and presidents, beginning with Ford and continuing through Carter and Reagan, had publicly supported competition and deregulation. The public interest lobby was not supportive of AT&T. Consumer activists, like Ralph Nader, disparaged the telephone monopoly and called for greater competition, especially supporting customer premise equipment, which would offer customers greater choice and freedom to use the telephone network as they wished. All of these disparate allies rallied around the banner of the deregulatory movement, which put them in the vantage point of appearing as reformers bent on undoing the abuses and privileges of the old regime. This deregulatory public ideology of the period was necessary to unite such disparate elements as MCI, its big business customers, IBM and the computer industry, and the public interest/Nader lobby. Together, they presented strong opposition to AT&T, and AT&T thus began its congressional lobbying and public education efforts in the weaker position. To illustrate AT&T's weak posture, opponents dubbed AT&T's bill (formally titled the Consumer Communications Reform Act [CCRA]) the "Bell Bill," indicating that CCRA was nothing more than protection for the special interest monopoly.

While the Bell bill became bogged down in committee hearings, AT&T did rally widespread initial support for CCRA with 175 congressmen and 17 senators cosponsoring the legislation. However, many felt the Bell bill to be so extreme in its anticompetitive provisions that USITA and CWA pulled back support, leaving AT&T in the untenable position of lacking strong public allies. This division among the traditional telephone industry reinforced the bill's image as a sop to AT&T, which greatly harmed any attempts to build public backing for AT&T's position. CCRA's anticompetition rigidity also offered opponents a rallying point. Opposition to the bill organized and grew, making AT&T's job more difficult and finally crushing any opportunity to produce a more moderate bill that would secure the regulated monopoly and the universal service standard.

The campaign in Congress was a dismal failure, as was the campaign to build public support for regulation. This stands in marked contrast to Vail's 1907–14 campaign, which successfully led to protective regulation (Long, 1962, 109–21). Why was AT&T so unsuccessful in the 1970s when it had been so successful in the early decades of the century? During the period of progressive reform, regulation was strongly backed by the public and business—there was a strong national consensus in support of regulation. In the 1970s, the tides had swung away from consensual support for regulation to strong support for deregulation. This time, AT&T did not have the public mood behind it. The opposition in the early 1900s of the independent telephone companies was limited, in spite of the fact they were dispersed nationally with numerous congressional allies. In contrast, almost all of big business opposed AT&T in the 1970s. Together they had support in Congress comparable to, if not stronger than, AT&T's support in the halls of legislature. Moreover, AT&T's tactics seemed heavy-handed and clumsy, which not only alienated leaders in Congress but hardened AT&T's poor public image as characterized by the derisive epithet "Ma Bell." The combination of these factors surely doomed AT&T's radical bill.

AT&T Relents: The Divestiture Agreement

Three events seemed to lead AT&T toward acceptance of competition and divestiture. First, AT&T's defeat in Congress shut off the legislative strategy. The only policy-making options open were legal and regulatory, and clearly AT&T had not fared well in those arenas over the years. Second, it appeared as if legal judgment might allow AT&T out of the boundary restrictions of the 1956 Consent Decree, which had prohibited AT&T entry into competitive markets. New Jersey's Federal Appeals Court had jurisdiction over the 1956 Consent Decree because this was where the 1949 case was filed. Court Judge Buinno issued a decision on September 3, 1981, suggesting that he favored allowing AT&T entry into computer markets, which the 1956 Consent Decree prohibited, but only through a separate subsidy for which the FCC had provided in *Computer II* for all common carriers except AT&T (Stone, 1989, 313; Temin with Galambos, 1987, 265). Third, the presiding judge of the DOJ's 1974 antitrust suit, Harold Greene, in a decision considering AT&T's petition to dismiss the case, hinted that he might decide against AT&T and for DOJ's position. AT&T lost on almost every point made in its dismissal motion, indicating a high probability of losing the case (Stone, 1989, 310–13; Temin with Galambos, 1987, 251–54).

Also motivating AT&T's willingness to divest and restructure was Assistant Attorney General William Baxter's willingness to negotiate a settlement out of court, where AT&T could at least control some outcomes that it was unable to control in Judge Greene's venue. AT&T's greatest fears were loss of Bell Laboratories and Western Electric, which Greene might divest from AT&T. Also, President de Butts had left office, to be replaced by Charles Brown. Leadership turnover provided a break with the old regime, which was locked into long-standing policy. New leadership, promoted through the ranks of the company, could more easily change policy direction.

Thus, AT&T entered into an agreement with the Department of Justice to divest and reorganize. That agreement was reached on January 8, 1982; the agreement, which was offered as a modification of the 1956 Consent Decree, was officially accepted by Judge Green with modification on August 24, 1982, and on July 8, 1983, Judge Greene approved with modification AT&T's reorganization plans, implementing the Modified Final Judgment (MFJ) (Stone, 1989, 320–32; Temin with Galambos, 1987, 268–91).

The Provisions of the MFJ

The Modified Final Judgment, as revised by Judge Greene, radically restructured not only AT&T but the entire telephone and telecommunications industry. The heart of the MFJ was the separation of competitive from natural monopoly services. First, AT&T was to divest itself of the local operating companies. Local telephone service was still considered a natural monopoly; long distance was now conceptualized as competitive. The 22 older local operating companies were to be reorganized into seven regional holding companies (RHCs), later known as the "Baby Bells." Second, AT&T would not only offer long distance services, but would retain control over its technology through retention of Western Electric and Bell Labs. Three, all licensing and supply agreements between Western Electric and the new RHCs were to be canceled, and the RHCs were to show no preference for Western Electric equipment. Fourth, AT&T would be prohibited from acquiring stock in any RHC. Fifth, the RHCs were to provide equal access to and interconnection with the local loop to any long distance provider, either AT&T or the SCCs, and to show no preference for AT&T. Sixth, the RHCs were forbidden from producing customer premise and other telecommunications equipment (although they could lease them to customers). Nor could they offer interexchange long distance and information (data processing) services. Seventh, recognizing the financial plight that the RHCs may see with the loss of long distance revenues, Judge Greene gave the Yellow Pages, a nonregulated service, to the RHCs. Similarly, they could enter other business markets if they were able to prove that they were not using their monopoly power within those markets. Finally, recognizing AT&T's great size, Greene prohibited AT&T from entering electronic publishing for seven years (Stone, 1989, 327–28, 330).

Early fallout from the MFJ was strongly negative; congressional leaders, especially Senator Robert Packwood of Oregon, chair of the Senate Commerce Committee, and Representative Tim Wirth of Colorado, chair of the House Subcommittee on Telecommunications of the Energy and Commerce Committee, offered separate, and conflicting, bills to preserve universal service. While neither was passed, they did indicate congressional pressures and concerns that would continue to mount in the future.

The Provisions of the Reorganization Plan

The reorganization plan would take effect January 1, 1984—after that time the old integrated AT&T network would be dissolved. In its place were the newly competitive AT&T and the local monopoly RHCs. Seven RHCs were created, each of approximately equal size. Each one alone would still stand among the nation's largest companies. They would be subdivided into local access transport areas (LATAs). Local service was within LATAs, as was some long distance. Further, as most LATAs stayed within state boundaries, intrastate but interLATA long distance was to be regulated by the state PUCs. An issue of concern for the states in the future would be whether or not to allow competition into these intraLATA markets. As things stood initially, the RHCs would provide intraLATA long distance.

Further, to help the RHCs develop their technologies, a research consortium styled after Bell Laboratories was to be created, called "Bellcore." Lastly, and significantly, Greene disallowed AT&T use of the "Bell" logo. This was given to the RHCs, Greene arguing that if both AT&T and its former subsidiaries used the old "Bell" logo, customer confusion would arise concerning the relationship between the new AT&T and the RHCs. To effect strict actual separation, there must be symbolic separation in the public's mind (Stone, 1989, 331–32).

Conclusion: Government–Business Relations—
First Steps Toward a Theory of Regulatory Policy Making

Chapter 1 outlined a perspective with which to begin to understand telecommunications policy. Two dimensions mapped the contours of the policy area: (1) AT&T's satisfaction with its market position, including its market share as well as profit level; and (2) government policy preferences, which ran from laissez-faire to nationalization. In the early part of the century, AT&T's threatened market position forced the company to seek a governmental solution when a market monopoly approach seemed impossible. AT&T was instrumental in motivating the government toward a regulatory approach.

However, over time, government policy contradictions between antitrust and regulation arose. Numerous factors allowed antitrust considerations to enter the governmental policy orbit around AT&T, including antimonopoly sentiment, New Deal ideology of government intervention into the economy, the economic loophole of the separations process, and technological developments. Through the mid-1950s AT&T was relatively successful in erecting a regulatory cocoon around itself, protecting the company from antitrust policies, which it feared would weaken its market position.

In the late 1950s, the FCC slowly began to allow antitrust-competitive concerns into its policy decisions regarding regulation of AT&T. Without the impetus from potential rivals of AT&T, it is unclear whether such a transformation in the policy regime would have occurred. Like AT&T, competitors might be satisfied or dissatisfied with their market position. AT&T, by seeking regulation and an accommodation with the independent telephone companies, helped foster a degree of satisfaction among those former rivals. Unforeseen was that new competitors would arise to challenge AT&T. These new rivals were naturally displeased with their market position—AT&T and the independents monopolized telecommunications. Further, since the policy regime used regulation to stabilize the market relationships of AT&T and the independents, these new rivals could not use regulatory logic to enter the market. They turned instead to antitrust, using it as a weapon against AT&T and its regulatory protectors. Thus, they had found a way to enter the market and protect their own toehold on that newly opened market. In the end they helped transform the government–AT&T relationship from one of regulation to one of antitrust concerns, with some regulation retained to constrict the muscle of the extremely large AT&T. Thus, while governmental change is instrumental in accounting for the developing relationship between AT&T and the government, government was in turn acted upon by these new rivals to AT&T.

Chapters 1 and 2 have focused on two themes crucial to building the theory presented in this book. The first of these themes is the multiple interest nature of regulatory policy making. For the most part, scholars now hold to some view of multiple interests, as opposed to the old single interest theories, such as interest group capture. The AT&T case is perhaps the best for winding up the issue of interest group capture.

Utility regulation is the special case where one would expect to find a single interest capturing the policy subsystem, and the AT&T case is the strongest of the utility cases because of the sheer size of the company, its national prominence, and its special relationship with the federal government. Even recognizing the power of AT&T, one must acknowledge that while it might have dominated regulatory policy making during certain periods, it certainly did not maintain dominance to the extent the interest group capture theories would propose. In fact, it is more the case that through separations and cross-subsidies from long distance to local operations (decisions that supported AT&T's regulated interests) a coalition was forged, of which AT&T was but one, albeit the crucial, element. Still, once challenged, even this mighty colossus and its coalition of support fell.

This issue of multiple interests is important for the development of the conditional effects theory, and especially its major component, the notion of relative resources, because only through the examination of several policy actors can one test the relative resources notion. In so far as the AT&T case is a good example of finding multiple interests where one might have traditionally expected to find only one major actor, whatever support we garner for the conditional effects theory in the following chapters will be bolstered.

The second theme relates to the nature of the policy debate, which in this realm is between equity and efficiency concerns. I have shown how the equity–efficiency debate resonates with the regulation–antitrust debate. Moreover, by spelling out the terms of this debate and relating it to the economics of telephone pricing, one can see the distributive consequences of regulation versus antitrust. Those distributive consequences are important in understanding the motivations of the several interests involved in this policy area and how they will respond to the choices before and decisions of the state public utility commissions. While multiple interests define *who* is involved in making policy, the distributive consequences tell us *why* they are involved, and the combination of who and why allows us to understand the composition and nature of the coalitions that are forged in the battles to make and implement public policy. The questions of who and why are thus answered in part in the present chapter. The following chapters go on to examine one of the core issues raised in this study, the nature of policy influence.

Notes

1. For a discussion of predation in telecommunications, see Kaserman and Mayo (1986). Economists have found little empirical support for predatory pricing. Generally, the theory now holds that if monopolies overcharge in their monopoly market, competitors will enter the market with lower prices, thereby eroding the market. Thus, anticipation of competition should preclude predatory pricing behavior (see Elzinga, 1970; Isaac and Smith, 1985; Koller, 1971). However, insofar as a monopoly market may have high entry barriers, for example through regulations, the monopoly may be protected in its controlled market, thereby keeping the threat of predation in other competitive markets alive.

2. The study was also referred to as the Walker report. The final FCC report watered down the investigation's proposals. It is reported in Federal Communications Commission (1939). A scholarly summary of the report that is consistent with the New Deal bias against the telephone company was published by staffer Danielian (1939).

3. The following is based primarily on Sichter (1977), Temin with Galambos (1987, 19–26), and Temin and Peters (1985a, 1985b).

4. The Supreme Court in 1930 actually began to require some kind of station-to-station costing formula in *Smith* v. *Illinois Bell*. However, the Court did not indicate exactly how costs were to be separated.

5. One reason for the government entering into the Consent Decree was a change in administration from Truman's Democratic one to Eisenhower's Republican one. Stone (1989, 77) argues that the Republicans viewed AT&T as a natural resource, and drastic restructuring would harm both the company and the nation, a significant departure from the Democratic view that AT&T was a monopoly that needed to be dismantled.

6. The Defense Department relied strongly on AT&T for satellite and other defense-related equipment and services, including the high-tech weapons facility at Sandia Laboratory. On the relationship between AT&T and DOD see Bolling (1983), Horwitz (1986, 128–29), and Soloman (1978).

7. The difficulty of the computer–communication distinction has continued since the FCC began *Computer III* in 1985.

8. The jury awarded MCI $600 million, which was trebled to $1.8 billion as required to by the Clayton Act.

9. The FCC reviewed the EXECUNET case and a similar service, SPRINT, in 1978 in light of the judicial ruling, finding that AT&T was correct in not having to interconnect with either service. AT&T appealed the decision into the Court of Appeals, and again it lost, taking its case to the Supreme Court. The Court denied certiorari, thereby letting the lower court's decision stand. This process was concluded in 1984.

10. Another post-EXECUNET controversy followed, ENFIA, the tariff structure proposed by AT&T to charge EXECUNET and SPRINT for the now mandatory interconnection. Controversy surrounded ENFIA from 1978, when AT&T initially filed it, to its conclusion in 1984. Throughout, the SCC offerings paid lower tariffs to the local telephone companies than AT&T did, allowing them to compete effectively with AT&T and erode AT&T's control of the long distance market (Stone, 1989, 258–60).

11. This section is based on Coll (1986, 93–102, 109–11, 242–53), Derthick and Quirk (1985, 98–105, 174–202, 256–57), Henck and Strassburg (1988, 204–15), Kahaner (1986, 128–33, 180–82), Stone (1989, 296–99), and Temin with Galambos (1987, 175–90).

3

Telephone Regulatory Policy in the American States, 1977–85

Introduction

In this chapter I begin the analysis of state telephone policy during the 1977–85 period. While the model tested in this chapter does not assume the conditional effects theory in its fully developed form, the analysis still departs from most past research on regulatory policy. Specifically, I begin to build the multiple-interest component of the conditional effects perspective. Considerable time will be spent discussing the nature of the resources of the active participants in this policy area, as well as their preferences along the equity–efficiency policy continuum.

A multiple-interest perspective is relatively recent and still somewhat uncommon among regulatory policy studies. Traditionally, regulatory environments have been viewed in simplistic terms, as the venerable interest group capture theories exemplify (Bernstein, 1955; Peltzman, 1976; Posner, 1974; Stigler, 1971). Similarly, in recent years some revisionists have built elegant, yet simplistic models of regulatory policy making, asserting legislative (congressional) control (Weingast and Moran, 1983; but see Moe, 1987). A smaller body of literature has begun to look at regulation within a more complex frame of reference, although these studies rely on very different theoretical approaches (Cohen, 1986; Meier, 1988; Moe, 1985; Scholz and Wei, 1986).

There are two major sets of actors in the telecommunications regulation policy subsystem: private interests and authoritative political decision makers. Private interests, often the classic interest group, include the telephone companies and residential and business users. Further, as I show below, residential consumers are not a monolithic class with one common interest—residential consumers comprise several distinct classes, particularly urban versus rural residents. And these residential classes sometimes come into conflict, just like telephone companies conflict at the federal level (although telephone company competition at the state level is not much of an issue for the provision of local telephone service). Moreover, business users sometimes divide into two classes, big and small businesses, with policy conflicts between them also possible. What distinguishes this study from past work is this distinction it makes among private interests, as well as its acknowledgment of multifaceted competition and conflict among business users and urban and rural residents.

Authoritative political decision makers include regulators, legislators, and executives. Much research is beginning to uncover an important role for politicians, legislators, and executives regarding regulatory policy. Legislatures are no longer viewed as capitulating to interest groups and allowing them to capture their regulators. Legislators have interest in regulatory policy insofar as their electoral coalitions find regulation a motivating issue. And in the days of public interest groups, the mass public may be mobilized over regulatory issues unlike the more quiescent days before the emergence of these types of groups. Further, the emergence of the public interest group, with attendant public support, has changed the legislative equation, whereby intense private interests are now challenged by these large, diffuse, but potentially electorally active publics. Intense private interests no longer command regulatory policy in the legislative chambers, and the legislature no longer allows capture. In this sense, the regulatory-electoral sectors now intersect, increasing the number of factors that legislators must account for when framing regulatory policy.

Much the same dynamic now affects the executive. Importantly, the rise of public concerns over regulation increases the incentives for state executives to influence regulatory policy. And given the peak position of the executive and the relatively greater permeability of legislatures to intense private interests, the executive generally speaks more as an advocate of broad concerns than of narrow private interest ones.

While legislatures and executives play important roles in building regulatory policy, so do the regulators. I argue that the regulators have independent impact on the course of policy. They are not merely the pawns of interest groups, though those interests may have considerable influence with regulators. Nor do their political principals, executives, and legislatures control them totally, though politicians might exert undeniable influence over the regulators. But they do so only under certain conditions, which I will specify later.

Regulators are important actors in their own right, with preferences about the nature of regulatory policy, and most importantly, under many circumstances, the institutional resources to promote those views and implement them into public policy. They are not the classic disinterested and nonpolitical public administrators, nor are they mere arbiters in a game of competing interests or politicians. They are political actors with the preferences, resources, and incentives to affect the course of public policy, although all the aforementioned factors, telephone companies, residential and business users, legislators and executives, may be incorporated by them when building public policy. Regulators make policy within a complex environment, feeling the pulls and tugs of numerous forces. Still, they are not weaklings easily pushed around; they may also push policy in the directions that they prefer.

The analysis in this chapter represents but a starting point leading to a more theoretically rich perspective. The major limit of this chapter's analysis is the view of regulatory policy outcomes as a linear combination of the influence of the policies of several competitors. The conditional effects perspective does not overtly appear in this chapter.

I begin with a description of the policy issues and trends over the 1977–85 period. A discussion of the nature of each actor's resources and policy preferences follows. The chapter concludes with a statistical test using multiple regression, pooled cross sectional–time series techniques, but we must wait until a later chapter for tests of the conditional effects hypotheses outlined in the introduction to this book.

Issues in State Telephone Regulation
in the Divestiture Era

On August 24, 1982, Federal Judge Harold Greene issued the Modified Final Judgment (MFJ) to the AT&T–Department of Justice consent decree of the previous January.[1] The consent decree and the MFJ altered drastically the character and composition of AT&T and the way telecommunications would be regulated in the United States.

One problem for state regulators was providing sufficient revenues for the new Bell Operating Companies (BOCs).[2] In the predivestiture era, large sums were diverted from interstate communications (interstate long distance) to local operations in the form of a cross-subsidy (see the discussion in chapter 2). This cross-subsidy helped promote the policy of universal service, a major goal of federal and state telephone regulators—that is, the provision of affordable access to all consumers. The long distance-to-local cross-subsidy prevented local rates from rising above an affordability threshold. With the divestiture of AT&T, the BOCs could no longer count on long distance revenues to subsidize their local operations.

One state-level response has been to raise rates, but it matters *whose* rates are raised. Raising residential (consumer) rates, some fear, will lead to residential dropoff of the system, thereby threatening the universal service goal. Raising local business rates, that is, using local businesses to cross-subsidize residents, might lead to bypass of the local network by large business users. Since large businesses provide a major portion of revenues to telephone systems, their dropoff might also eventually lead to higher residential rates. The crux of the dilemma, then, is to raise rates while maintaining affordability and countering the bypass threat.

Two policy decisions are especially crucial in this regard, residential flat rates and the ratio of residential-to-business rates. Each presents different opportunities and limits on bureaucratic influence and political control. Data on state rates, the policy of interest, consist of a pooled cross–sectional time series (1977–85) for each state.

Residential Flat Rates

Telephone rates across states are difficult to compare because the states do not follow a uniform rate structure. For residential rates most states group residents into rate classes, the classes usually determined by the size of the community in which the resident lives. But these residential rate classes present us with important comparabilities. All states have a sliding rate structure, whereby rates in more populous areas are higher than in less populous areas. Hence, comparison can and should be made only across similar rate classes. The first variable of interest is the monthly residential flat rate in the largest population category (urban) corrected for inflation.[3] I focus on this rate class because it usually affects more people than any other category, making it among the most visible and politically charged.[4]

Table 3.1 details trends in urban residential flat rates from 1977 to 1985. Inspection of the average rate across the states indicates rates creeping upward. In 1977, the average flat rate totaled $9.31 a month. It hovered in the $9 to $10 range until 1981, about a year before divestiture was announced, when the rate slipped over the $10-per-month barrier to $10.19. With divestiture's announcement in 1982, and possibly in expectation of divestiture's impact on state rate policy, these urban residential flat rates jumped $0.64 to $10.83. They continued to rise at a significant pace, adding over a dollar a month in 1983 to $11.87, and almost another two dollars over the next two years to a 1985 total of $13.85 (1984 figures are excluded because the data source, the National Association of Regulatory Utility Commissioners, did not collect rate data that year).

When viewed from this vantage point, rates clearly show a pattern of increase at a pace to rouse public fears. From 1977 to 1985, the residential flat rate increased by almost 50 percent, or around 6 percent a year. However, the rate of increase during the postdivestiture period of 1982–85 was far greater. Rates rose less than one dollar from 1977 to 1981, or less than 2 percent a year. From 1981 to 1985 rates rose $3.66, or about 9 percent a year—a quadrupling in the rate of increase.

Inspection of the raw rate increases is suspect, however. The economy inflated during this period, although the rate of inflation did not match that of the previous ten years. Using 1977 as a baseline, the 1985 equivalent of 1977 dollars was 1.775. That is, from 1977 to 1985, the economy inflated by about 77.5 percent, or about 9.7 percent a year. This inflation rate is almost double that of the residential rate increase.

Detrending the flat rate with the inflation rate gives us a better picture of the actual consumer cost of telephone service. Viewed this way, telephone rates hardly increased. Because of the very high inflation rates of the late 1970s, plus the comparatively modest rate increases during that period, real telephone rates fell about 27 percent from 1977 to 1981. While this decline is partially attributable to inflation, the long-standing policy of cross-subsidization from long distance to local service, plus efficiency gains through innovation, also help

Table 3.1

Trends in Urban Residential Flat Rates, 1977–85

Year	Uncorrected		Inflation-corrected		
	Mean	sd	Mean	sd	n
1977	9.31	1.69	9.31	1.69	50
1978	10.04	2.12	9.33	1.97	49
1979	9.45	1.77	7.89	1.48	48
1980	9.71	2.11	7.14	1.48	48
1981	10.19	2.96	6.79	1.97	48
1982	10.83	2.70	6.80	1.70	48
1983	11.87	2.87	7.22	1.75	50
1985	13.85	3.57	7.80	2.01	47
All	10.67	2.91	7.79	2.00	392*

*Includes four cases for 1984.

account for this real rate reduction.

With the onset of divestiture in 1982, real rates ceased their slide and began to inch upward. From 1981 to 1985, rates rose a full dollar, or about 14.5 percent, if we use 1981 figures as the base—a rate of 3.6 percent per year above the inflation rate. While such a real rate increase is not very steep, and is considerably lower than divestiture's foes predicted, it still has the ability to mount greatly in the long term.

Another trend is noticeable in these data. Across the years the difference in state rates for urban residents began to become more pronounced, as seen in the standard deviations. Whether one inspects the raw rates or their inflation-detrended counterparts, by divestiture in 1982 a greater spread in state rates had become apparent (this trend is somewhat less visible with the corrected data). In other words, state rate making was growing increasingly dissimilar.

As I will illustrate in the following pages, this growing dissimilarity was a function of state politics impacting rate policy. While the political system always affected rate policy, divestiture altered the composite of forces affecting rates, and as that mix of forces varied from state to state, policy outcomes began to differentiate.

One can get a sense of this differentiation by turning these data around and asking, have all state urban rates changed the same way?

The answer is a resounding no. States can be grouped into three sets: those that allowed rates to rise, to stay relatively stable, or to decline. Comparing the uncorrected rates between 1977 and 1985 shows us that most states were allowing rates to increase, but some were forcing stability or declines onto these rates.

For comparative purposes, let us assume that increases greater than one dollar imply increasing rates, rates changing less than one dollar (either up or down) indicate stable rates, and those declining more than one dollar mark deflating rates. Of the 47 states for which we have data for both years, 40 (85 percent) allowed rates to increase a dollar or more, six held rates relatively constant, and one state (Delaware) actually forced a decline in uncorrected dollars. Thus, these computations indicate a general upward movement in rates, but again one must recall that these increases are not corrected for inflation.

Correcting for inflation presents us with a more varied picture of rate increases across the states. Now the largest category becomes those states forcing declines—fully 28 of 47 states (59.6 percent) promoted real cost rate declines. Half as many states held rates somewhat stable (14, or 29.8 percent), while only five allowed rates to climb in real terms. In other words, only five states (Kentucky, New Mexico, Oregon, West Virginia, and Wisconsin) allowed the residential cost for telephone service to increase at rates greater than inflation; most states either held rates somewhat close to the inflation rate, or more commonly, forced telephone companies to accept rates that were lower than the rate of inflation.

However, while customers may respond to actual (or even inflation-corrected) rates, these rates are relatively meaningless to policy making unless they are placed into the larger context of rates structures. If, as I have been arguing, that telephone rate policy has been strongly redistributive, and divestiture has threatened that redistributive formula of intergroup cross-subsidies, then it becomes more meaningful to inspect changes in rate structures as they relate to these important cross-subsidies. It will be over rate structures more than absolute rate levels that political debate and policy solutions will revolve. In fact, because of the highly intertwined nature of rates concerning the major customer classes (urban residents, business, and rural residents), altering any one group's rates affects the relative rates of the other groups—that is, the rate structure is modified. In this and the next two chapters I investigate the business-to-residential component of the rate structure.

Relative Residential and Business Rates

The business-to-residential cross-subsidy raises the classical political issue of redistribution and evokes the tensions that divestiture insinuated into state telephone rate making. One way to deal with high or increasing residential rates is to shove that rate burden onto someone else. Businesses become natural targets. Taxing businesses offers a simple solution to meet the economic needs of residents. Such redistributive issues are often easily sold to voters and may mobilize voter support more easily than purely technical and complex issues; hence, politicians may be under great pressure to redistribute. Lack of political discretion in managing redistributive issues may force politicians to limit bureaucratic input. Bureaucrats are less sensitive to the election needs of politicians and might not pursue policies that aid politicians in that electoral quest. In this area, the PUCs may be very fearful of bypass, and thus prefer policies that limit the burden on business. That position may run counter to the electoral needs of politicians; consequently, bureaucratic influence may be muted.

While this rate issue includes technical considerations, especially those emanating from the base rate levels of the affected customer classes and the need to balance universal service and affordability with the revenue needs of the telephone companies, the consumer-to-business rate ratio evokes important redistributive concerns. Therefore, one can consider this to be a mixed issue, one with both technical and redistributive elements. The consumer-to-business ratio is expressed as monthly urban residential flat rates divided by monthly urban business flat rates. This variable is similar in construction and meaning to one that Berry (1979) used in his study of electric utility rates. In the following discussion this becomes the central variable of interest because of its direct relation to the policy divisions in the states and its relation to the theoretical concepts we will be considering.

Trends in the ratio, defined as the urban residential flat rate divided by the urban business flat rate, differ from those discerned for the flat rates. First of all, the ratio seems hardly to have budged over the 1977–85 period (see Table 3.2). Across all years and every year, residential rates compared with business rates have remained slightly greater than one-third. Further, while there exists an ample range in the ratio across the states, across the years state variability in the ratio has remained remarkably stable, with standard deviations ranging only

Table 3.2

Trends in Relative Residential and Business Rates

Year	Mean Ratio	Standard Deviation	n
1977	.379	.038	36
1978	.389	.055	37
1979	.376	.053	36
1980	.376	.059	36
1981	.372	.063	36
1982	.360	.040	35
1983	.360	.048	36
1985	.379	.045	36
All	.375	.051	291*

*Includes three cases for 1984.

from .04 to .06 and displaying no trend over time. These data indicate that while flat rates have been escalating, states have retained the old, predivestiture pricing formulas, whereby businesses pay more than residents. Yet, business has not been forced to pick up any more of the cost of operating the state systems to offset the lessened revenue transfers from the federal level to the states as a consequence of divestiture. That the states have been so conservative in terms of these intrastate rate ratios indicates that perhaps one should look elsewhere for major change and adaptation in state policy responses to divestiture—perhaps focusing on new rates structures, as Teske (1990) does.

While at the aggregate level the ratio appears stationary, however, disaggregating by state shows considerable alteration in state rate structures over time. I do this by comparing the ratio of each state in 1977 and 1985. Again, let us group the states in three sets, those that required greater relative residential-to-business rates, those that maintained the old rate structure, and those that required a greater relative business burden. Let us define the first group as those that have increased the ratio by 3 percent or more (.03 on the ratio), the second group as those for which the ratio stayed within a plus or minus 3 percent range, and the third group as those states that have decreased the ratio by 3 percent. One finds 10 states of 34 (29.4 percent) with data at both time points (most of the missing states did not offer flat rate service to urban businesses) falling into this category. A relatively similarly sized group (8, or 23.5 percent) of the states fostered a greater relative business burden from 1977 to 1985, while the remaining 16 states (47.1 percent) held the rate structure relatively stable. Thus, about one-half of the states found divestiture pressures motivating some kind of restructuring in the urban residential-to-business rate ratio, though as many states promoted anti-business as pro-business policies.

For instance, in 1977 the state with the highest ratio was North Dakota, at .50, and the one with the lowest was Montana, at .31. In 1985, the state with the highest ratio was Arkansas, with .48, while Colorado and Montana registered the lowest rate, at .30. The states displaying the greatest increases in the ratio were Kansas (+.09), Arkansas (+.07), and Texas (+.07). The greatest declines in the ratio were found in North Dakota (−.10), New Mexico (−.06), and Indiana, Iowa, and Nevada (−.05). One of the tasks of this study is to account for these varying state responses to divestiture.

Accounting for State Telephone Policy: The Impact of Bureaucrats, Politicians, and Interest Groups

The previous section documented the changes over time and differences across states with regard to telephone rates. In this section I develop the hypotheses and operational measures to test the idea that regulatory policy is constructed within a complex, multiple interest environment. Also, here more than elsewhere I focus on the impact of bureaucrats in the telephone regulatory process.

Conceptualizing Bureaucratic Resources

A major finding of my research is that both the public and regulators have considerable impact on regulatory policy. How regulators define the public interest tells us much about their policy preferences. As regulation usually involves some kind of balancing between provider and consumer interests, regulators will be sensitive to public interests, either as the public itself defines those interests, or perhaps more commonly when issues are complex, as the regulators define what is in the best interests of the public. Considering the crucial role that I give to regulators in this research, I will here discuss in some detail regulators' (bureaucrats') influence over public policy.

Major statements about the nature of bureaucratic influence on the policy process abound (Bernstein, 1955; Berry, 1979; Gormley, 1983, 160–72; Meier, 1980, 1985, 1987, 1988; Mitnick, 1980; Rourke, 1969; Scholz and Wei, 1986; Wood, 1988). While scholars provide us with lists of bureaucratic resources, these lists rarely are integrated into a general framework. As the literature implies and this study will assume, the impact of bureaucratic resources resides in their ability to produce (1) capabilities that politicians do not possess and/or (2) bureaucratic power bases independent of the power bases of politicians.

Bureaucratic Capabilities

Bureaucrats are better able to make use of detail and information than politicians. Detail and information may pertain to bureaucratic performance, clientele attitudes, or technical criteria. Bureaucratic discretion over the collection and utilization of information, what information to relay to politicians, and the form it takes, may heighten the policy impact of information. Hence information might better serve the needs of bureaucrats than the needs of politicians, and bureaucrats may be able to manipulate information to increase their advantages in the policy-making process.

Independent Power Bases

Ties with interest groups, public support, and/or nonpartisan professionalism may all serve as power bases independent of those of politicians. Supportive interest groups (even capturing ones) might pressure politicians in behalf of favored bureaucracies and programs. Public esteem may limit the opportunity and extent to which politicians may criticize the bureaucracy. Lastly, some bureaucracies might appear "above politics," perhaps because of their technical orientation, incorruptible and fairminded reputation, or sense of public "mission." Such a public umbrella may interfere with political attempts at control, thereby allowing increased bureaucratic influence on public policy. The combined impact of information control and independent power might allow construction of policy somewhat more in accord with bureaucratic preferences, goals, and styles.

Based on the literature and the above outline, three resources may increase information control or provide an independent base of power:

personnel, scope of agency powers, and organizational structure (Meier, 1980, 1987, 1988, 65–73; Mitnick, 1980, 13; Rourke, 1969).[5]

1. Personnel refers to the size and expertise of staffs. Large and expert staffs are better able to collect and utilize information. Further, such staffs have greater capacity to generate technical information. The collection of large amounts of often technical information may give the agency an information advantage over politicians, who often lack the capacity to utilize technical information. Politicians therefore are apt to rely on the judgments of bureaucrats when trying to utilize technical information.

2. Scope of agency powers are those powers that the legislature grants to the agency. Legislative grants of authority may allow some level of bureaucratic discretion. Legislatures often provide agencies with broad discretionary powers because of legislative inability to foresee and deal with every contingency (Bryner, 1987). Discretion often leads to bureaucratic influence over the definition of the problem at hand, and broad grants of authority help legitimate bureaucratic actions. Granting an agency broad discretionary powers might indicate lack of legislative interest in the details of policy. All of these reasons might allow the bureaucracy greater latitude and influence in the policy process.

3. A major defining characteristic of organizational structure is the level of complexity. Organizational complexity refers to an agency's degree of internal specialization and routinization. Complex organizations are composed of a number of different levels and units within levels. Complexity provides a degree of specialization—a division of labor—that enhances the agency's ability to tackle large, difficult tasks and to understand and utilize technical information. Further, organizational complexity forces a degree of routinization on agency procedures and relations among agency personnel. These routines—standard operating procedures—often limit the politicians' ability to intrude into agency operations. When faced with political pressures, the affected agency, if organizationally complex, might be able to withstand pressures by "going by the book," or by using these routines to stall until the pressure eases. Importantly, operation of these routines might provide the appearance of bureaucratic responsiveness to political pressure. The appearance of responsiveness derives from a sense of wheels being set in motion even though nothing more than symbolic action might have been taken. Hence, complexity increases agency informa-

tion advantages, and routines may deflect or mitigate political pressures on the agency.

Measuring Bureaucratic Resources

In this section, I present the operationalizations of the variables used to measure bureaucratic resources and discuss their expected relationships with the telephone policies. Table 3.3 presents the exact operationalizations of each variable used in the analysis.

Personnel

The number of PUC employees (EMPLOY) measures personnel levels.[6] Table 3.4 displays some descriptive statistics on PUC personnel levels across the years. The average PUC numbered merely 169 employees, not a very high level considering the scope of most PUC missions. Across the states there exists great variability in the size of PUCs, with the smallest totaling a paltry seven employees, and the largest, California, fielding nearly a thousand. Further, one may consider most state PUCs understaffed because (1) they are multipurpose agencies, regulating a number of areas beyond telecommunications, which may include electric, transportation, water, and commerce; and (2) single-purpose federal agencies (SEC, NLRB), often with two to three times the staff of even the largest state PUC and perhaps ten times the staff of the average PUC, complain of understaffing. Such a perspective should highlight the importance of staff size to the state PUCs—small staff growth may have great impact on productivity at the agency level. Table 3.4 indicates that over time the state PUCs have grown from about 161 employees in 1977 to about 178 in 1985. This represents a growth rate of slightly over 10 percent; yet even growing at such a pace may not provide the PUCs with large enough staffs to be truly effective regulatory bodies.

Agency Powers

PUCs are primarily economic regulatory agencies. Hence, among their most important powers might be control of the economic sectors over which they have jurisdiction. These powers might often include regulation of markets, provision of exclusive contracts to service providers,

Table 3.3

Variables Used in the Analysis

BELL   Percentage of telephones in the Bell network.
                  Source: NARUC, 1977–85a.

BUSIPCT   Percentage of state's telephones that are business as opposed to residential.
                  Source: FCC Statistics of Common Carriers.

CCAUSE   Number of members of Common Cause per 10,000.
                  Source: McFarland, 1984,52.

COMPLEX   Number of the following PUC possessions/characteristics:
                  1 = a research section or permanent research staff,
                  2 = a research library,
                  3 = a separately staffed public information office,
                  4 = whether or not administrative law judges and hearing examiners are full-time employees,
                  5 = whether the staff is covered under civil service or merit protection,
                  6 = whether data-processing and computer equipment are used.
                  Source: NARUC, 1977–85a.

CONIN   PUC is covered under conflict of interest provisions.
                  1 = covered, 0 = not covered.
                  Source: NARUC, 1977–85a.

ELECTION   If the PUC commissioners are elected or not.
                  1 = elected, 0 = not elected.
                  Source: NARUC, 1977–85a.

EMPLOY   Number of employees in the PUC.
                  Source: NARUC, 1977–85a.

EXARM   PUC is an arm of the executive.
                  1 = is an arm, 0 = is not an arm.
                  Source: NARUC, 1977–85a.

GPARTY   Party of the governor
                  –1 = Republican, 0 = Independent, 1 = Democrat.
                  Source: Book of the States, 1977–85.

GPOWER   Index of gubernatorial power
                  Source: Beyle, 1983.

GRASS   Grassroots advocacy activity level
                  1 = high, 0 = low.
                  Source: Gormley, 1983,40.

LARM   PUC is an arm of the legislature.
                  0 = not an arm, 1 = is an arm.
                  Source: NARUC, 1977–85a.

LICEN   Number of the following licensing powers that the PUC possesses:
                  1 = to initiate telephone service,
                  2 = to lay transmission lines,
                  3 = to lay distribution lines,
                  4 = to operate other types of plants,
                  5 = to allow abandonment of facilities and services,
                  6 = to issue indeterminate permits,
                  7 = to allocate unincorporated territory among the telephone utilities.
                  Source: NARUC, 1977–85a.

Table 3.3 *(continued)*

LPARTY	Legislative party control Average percentage Democrat of the two chambers. *Source:* Book of the States, 1977–85.
LRULE	Legislative committee rule review 0 = no rule review power, 1 = review authority must be given to a committee, 2 = review authority also must be general, that is, not limited to a specific agency or program, 3 = review authority has to include the possibility of authoritative action on agency regulations. *Source:* Book of the States, 1977–85.
LSAL	Legislative salaries, annual, corrected for inflation. *Source:* Book of the States, 1977–85.
PENET	Percentage of households in the state with telephone service. *Source:* Statistical Abstract of the United States, 1977–85.
POV	Percentage of the state's population living below the poverty level. *Source:* Statistical Abstract of the United States, 1977–85.
PROXY	Proxy advocacy activity level 1 = high, 0 = low. *Source:* Gormley, 1983,40.
SAFE	Numerical count of safety aspects that can be regulated by PUC.
SOUTH	South 1 = Confederate state, 0 = not a Confederate state.
TIME	Time regulations between leaving the PUC and beginning employment in a regulated firm 1 = time regulations, 0 = no time regulations. *Source:* NARUC, 1977–85.
URBAN	Percentage of the state's population living in urban areas. *Source:* Statistical Abstract of the United States, 1977–85.

erection of barriers to market entry, terms of provider behavior, standard accounting and assessment procedures, and so forth. In many cases, these types of regulations may be viewed as protections of the regulated industry. These are often associated with licenses and permits to operate, as well as guarantees of reasonable rates of return for the regulated enterprises. To measure the economic regulatory power of the public utility commissions, I total how many of the following seven licenses, certificates, and/or permits the PUC can require (LICEN) with regard to telephone companies: (1) to initiate telephone service, (2) to lay transmission lines, (3) to lay distribution lines, (4) to operate other types of plants, (5) to allow abandonment of facilities and services, (6) to issue indeterminate permits, and (7) to allocate unincorporated territory among the telephone utilities.

The average PUC held of these powers only a modest number,

Table 3.4

Descriptive Statistics on Bureaucratic Variables

	Mean		
Year	Personnel	Agency Powers	Agency Complexity
1977	161	3.5	2.9
1978	161	3.5	2.9
1979	166	3.5	2.9
1980	165	3.5	3.1
1981	167	3.5	3.4
1982	168	3.5	3.5
1983	177	3.5	3.5
1984	178	3.6	3.5
1985	178	3.6	3.5
All	169	3.5	3.2

3.5. However, the range in the number of powers held was quite wide, from none to all seven. Across the years, these powers granted to the PUCs have remained relatively stable, with the average inching up slightly from 3.5 in 1977 to 3.6 in 1985. Although telephone regulation became a more salient and demanding chore of the PUCs in the wake of divestiture, state politicians did not feel it necessary to increase PUC powers. It appears almost as if the politicians were reserving their right to intervene in telecommunications regulatory policy by not granting the PUCs increased regulatory powers. In light of this stability, the modest growth in PUC personnel may be more symbolic than effective.

Organizational Complexity

Organizational complexity (COMPLEX) is an index that counts how many out of six offices, separate units, and/or capabilities one finds in the PUC. Though COMPLEX includes units that may enhance expertise, COMPLEX is conceptually distinct from expertise. Possession of supposed expert units (e.g., research staff units) does not tell us how many people are located there or whether they possess technical skills. Further, lack of such units does not preclude location of expert staff within other units. One is more likely, however, to find technically proficient and expert staff in large organizations. To determine the

PUCs, level of organizational complexity I totaled how many of the following units and/or specialized capabilities they possessed: (1) a research section or permanent research staff, (2) a research library, (3) a separately staffed public information office, (4) whether or not administrative law judges and hearing examiners are full-time employees, (5) whether the staff is covered under civil service or merit protection, (6) whether data-processing and computer equipment are used.

The average PUC held 3.2 of these six capabilities. As found for personnel levels and agency powers, the state PUCs vary tremendously in their organizational complexity, with some holding none of these special units to some holding all six. However, somewhat more like personnel and unlike powers, the average level of organizational complexity increased marginally over the years. In the beginning of the series, the average PUC held only 2.9 of these units/capabilities. By 1985, the average held 3.5.

However, the increase in complexity came before the increase in personnel. The major jump in complexity commenced between 1979 and 1981, while the personnel jump began between 1982 and 1983. There are two possible explanations for these trends: (1) personnel were added because of the growing complexity of the organizations (that is, complexity became the reason for adding personnel—new units and capabilities required more people for the PUC to function optimally), and (2) these trends may be independent. Personnel growth may be partially a response to the new exigencies caused by divestiture, not agency complexity. Perhaps the long-term trend toward federal deregulation in other sectors might have impelled greater complexity among the PUCs as they added tasks once served at the federal level. Intensive case studies are probably required to sort out these differing explanations—they are of only tangential interest to our main focus, however.

Other scholars have used similar types of data to measure the organizational attributes of the PUCs, although very little attention has been paid to agency powers, while they often note its theoretical importance. Further, the complexity measure is unique, although others have relied on some of its components. To give some sense of the relative uniqueness of these aspects of PUC capabilities, I correlated the variables, finding a Pearson Product Moment correlation of -.05 and -.05 of licensing powers with complexity and employment, and a correlation between employment and complexity of .38. Only the third is significant at any conventional cutoff (here at the .01 level), but I am not willing to argue that such a modest correlation testifies to a strong similarity between these two variables. Although related, the correlation is too modest for us to suggest that employment and complexity are measuring the same thing. Further, as I will show, these three variables do not even display similar relationships with political system attributes.

Politicians: Legislatures and Executives

Politicians need access to the bureaucratic decision-making process as well as information capabilities if they are to affect bureaucratic decisions. First, politicians must have access to the bureaucracy before they can influence bureaucratic decision making. This is often expressed formally: whether an agency is an arm of the executive or legislative branch indicates the accessibility of the bureaucrat to the politician. Other forms that access may take include requiring bureaucracies to submit reports, limiting control over budgets,[7] and appointing high-level bureaucrats.

To be effective, however, politicians must be able to compete with the often highly developed bureaucratic information capabilities. They do so by developing their own information and intelligence capabilities. Strong committee systems, well-developed staffs, and rule-review powers are indications of a political information capability. Thus, through access and capability politicians are able to translate their preferences into bureaucratic control.

Governors and state legislators must be able to translate their preferences into bureaucratic control. Higher levels of institutional resources increase the ability of governors and legislatures to convert preferences into control. This resembles Carmines' theory of the mediating impact of legislative capability in translating public preferences into policies (Carmines, 1974).

The formal relationship between politicians and bureaucrats is more a relational than an institutional resource. Formal relationships create expectations, routines, and in the context of legislative-executive conflict, questions of turf. In some states, executive intrusion may be prohibited, in others the legislature may be blocked, and in still others, both legislature and governor may share formal duties over the PUCs. Lastly, states may restrict the formal ties of both the legislature and the executive. These may be the truly "independent" PUCs. Hence, formally defined relations between the PUCs and the political branches may determine to whom the PUCs will be attentive. Even with high levels of institutional resources, politicians may be restricted in their influence if their branch has no formal ties with the PUC. To complete this discussion, we also need to know something about the direction of preferences—whether the politicians side with residential interests or those of business.

Operational Measures

Party may serve as one proxy for the regulatory policy preferences of politicians. The natural redistributive leanings of Democrats will make them more favorable to a smaller rate ratio than Republicans, whose natural constituency is business. Thus, states with Republican governors and/or state legislatures will see a larger ratio than states with Democratic politicians. I operationalize Governor's party (GPARTY) with a simple party variable. Legislative party control (LPARTY) is operationalized as the average percentage Democrat of the two chambers.

Beyle's (1983) Index of Gubernatorial Powers (GPOWER) is used to measure gubernatorial capacity. The more formal powers at the governor's disposal, the greater the governor's ability to influence the PUCs. Further, these institutional resources may help governors transfer the perceived political pressures that they feel onto the PUC. Hence, I expect that greater gubernatorial powers will lead to a smaller ratio.

Two variables measure legislative capability: legislative salaries (LSAL) and an Index of Committee Rule Review (LRULE) (Ethridge, 1981).[8] Legislative salaries measures one dimension of legislative professionalism (Grumm, 1969), and Chubb (1985) argues that legislative salaries is the best available measure of legislative professionalism. More professional legislatures should not only be concerned with their impact on policy, but also with public pressures, and they may be more able to convert these pressures into policy. Thus, higher salaries should covary with a smaller ratio. The variable is the yearly salary, corrected for inflation.[9]

Professional legislatures are also more likely to take an active part in the regulatory process, perhaps interceding in some proceedings and/or strictly overseeing the policies that regulators formulate. Ideally, a measure of legislative activity is desirable in rate cases. However, since such data are unavailable, I rely on a surrogate: committee rule review.

Committee rule review provides the legislature with an avenue through which it can intrude into the bureaucratic policy-making environment. The variable counts the powers the committee system possesses. While this variable relates to rule review, my concern is with rate making. At best, then, this variable indirectly measures the activity of the legislature in rate-making cases. My belief here is that legislatures that use this rule review power are also more likely to try to influence rate making. For instance, this intrusive legislative participation in rule making may inform bureaucrats of legislative intent not only over rules, but over acceptable rates, as well. As I will show, the rule-review variable has some statistical power, supporting these assumptions. Therefore, since legislators feel public pressures through the election process, one should find greater rule-review powers promoting a lower ratio.

Lastly, I measure the formal relationship between the PUCs and politicians with two dummy variables: whether the PUC is formally an arm of the executive (EXARM) or legislative (LARM) branch. These are not inverse variables because some PUCs are the arm of neither and some are considered an arm of both.[10] Whether a PUC is an arm of one branch or the other may determine to whom it feels it should be more responsive. This relationship may enable politicians to translate public concerns into policy: I expect both variables to foster a lower ratio. In summary, other than for partisan differences, all of the political variables should promote a lower residential-to-business ratio.

Politicians and Bureaucrats

Do particular political characteristics lead to particular bureaucratic structures? For instance, do more capable legislatures more greatly endow their bureaucracies, with the idea that the greater capability of the politicians will enable them to control these more powerful agencies? Or is it that less capable political branches create more powerful bureaucracies to ensure government's ability to regulate and/or to limit the possibility of interest group capture?

To address this question, I correlated the political structure measures with the three measures of bureaucratic capabilities. They are displayed in Table 3.5. Generally, there is no consistent relationship

Table 3.5

Pearson Product Moment Correlations among Political, Interest Group, and Bureaucratic Characteristics, 1977–85

	Personnel Powers	Agency Powers	Agency Complexity
Leg. Salaries	.64**	−.21**	.39**
Leg. Rule Review	−.12*	−.03	.04
Leg. Arm	−.01	.08	−.06
Leg. Party	.03	.02	−.05
Gov. Power	.20**	−.26**	.05
Exec. Arm	−.13*	−.11	.07
Gov. Party	−.06	−.01	−.16**
Time	.20**	−.27**	.29**
Conflict of Int.	.28**	.00	.17**
Bell %	.06	.03	−.16**
Business %	−.12**	−.20**	−.16**
Common Cause	.08	−.46**	−.11
Proxy	.06	−.32**	−.10
Grass	.04	.02	.07
Election	−.15**	−.01	−.25**
Penetration	.14	−.37**	.07
Urbanization	.32**	−.33**	.13*
Poverty	−.11**	.17*	−.31**

*Significant at .05 level; ** significant at .01 level.

between political and bureaucratic characteristics. Strong politicians do not create strong bureaucracies, nor do they seem to create weak ones either. Of the 21 possible correlations, only eight were significant at the .05 level or better. Only personnel was related to more than half of the political variables (four out of seven), while agency powers and complexity were related to only two apiece. Further, only one political variable was correlated to all three bureaucratic variables—legislative salaries. But while well-paid legislatures grant PUCs more personnel and greater levels of complexity, they restrict PUC regulatory powers. For the most part, then, politicians do not create bureaucracies in their image, nor do they create bureaucracies as reverse images. These findings suggest a more complex relationship between politicians and bureaucrats, and some of the complexity of that relationship might affect regulatory policy outcomes.

Private and Public Interest Groups

As with politicians, interest groups, whether of the special- or public-interest variety, must have access to bureaucrats and be able to utilize information about policy. Access may be provided directly—for instance, through public interveners (Gormley, 1983). Other times the revolving door provides direct access points (Cohen, 1986; Gormley, 1979), as may ex parte contacts. Many states restrict these forms of access, however. Access may also be forthcoming indirectly, as politicians are used to impress interest preferences onto the bureaucrats. This type of indirect access derives from the interests' ability to affect political careers and election campaigns. Further, some interests possess information that bureaucrats find useful. In some instances, when bureaucratic agencies are not well staffed and programs are highly technical, expertise and information come directly from interests, especially special and private interests. Most usually, private interests possess information and electorally based access (through campaign contributions), while public interest groups possess access through public mobilization and/or public interveners. However, public interests are often information-poor about technical matters, and information-rich about public preferences.

Regulatory policy has traditionally been viewed as an arena of interest group influence, sometimes even capture. Three sets of interests may affect telephone regulatory policy outcomes: the telephone companies and business and residential telephone users (and their advocates).

Private Interests

The local telephone companies are major players in the regulatory subsystem. Their primary interest concerns profits (which are guaranteed through the regulatory system) and increasing their revenue base (which divestiture threatens). However, the threat of bypass may lead them to side with their large business customers and favor a larger ratio. Another private interest with the potential for influencing rate policy consists of local businesses, and insofar as local businesses cross-subsidize residential users, business-residential conflict over rates may arise, and a business–telephone company alliance may be forged.

Interest group influence over regulatory bodies may be felt through (1) the revolving door[11]; (2) formal and informal relationships between the interest and the bureaucrat; and (3) the resources of interest groups.

1. Direct measurement of the revolving door is not possible because we lack data on career patterns after departure from the PUCs. But we can measure the potential for the revolving door with this dummy variable: whether or not there are time restrictions between leaving the PUC and finding employment with a regulated firm (TIME).
2. I measure regulation of formal relations between the telephone companies (the regulated interest) and the PUC with a dummy variable of whether or not the PUC was subject to a conflict of interest provision (CONIN). Both TIME and CONIN should be associated with a lower ratio.
3. I measure BOC resources as the percentage of a state's telephones in the Bell system—Bell's market share (BELL). As market share increases, so does the power of the BOC in the regulatory subsystem; hence, the ratio should be bigger.

Finally, one must consider the role of business customers. Recall that the dependent variable is a ratio of business to residential rates; hence, the major source of conflict might not be between consumers and the telephone companies, but between the different customer classes. To assess the relative importance of business versus residential customers I computed the percentage of telephones within the state that belong to business. I hypothesize that the greater this percentage, the more influence business customers will have over the PUCs, and accordingly, the greater the ratio.

Public Interests

The interest environment of the PUC includes public interest groups (PIRGs) as well. PIRG impact increased as the regulatory process was opened to the public, as public interest and intensity in regulatory issues rose, and as PIRG organizations developed (Gormley, 1983; McFarland, 1984). Like the case for private interests, the resources and activity of PIRGs might be important in their ability to influence the regulatory process.

To measure PIRG-related activity, I use Gormley's proxy and grassroots-advocacy variables (Gormley, 1983, 40). Both were based on a

1979 survey of all PUCs, and the survey queried PUC commissioners as to the perceived level of proxy and grassroots-advocate activity in regulatory proceedings. Each variable (PROXY, GRASS) is a dummy variable distinguishing between high and low levels of activity, as Gormley indicates. I expect both variables to lead to a smaller ratio.

I also indirectly measure PIRG organizational resources with a variable that has been used in related research: Common Cause membership per 10,000 (CCAUSE). Figures on Common Cause membership by state are found in McFarland (1984, 52). A good theoretical justification for using the Common Cause figures as I am doing here can be found in Kau and Rubin (1982). Similar measures of PIRG activity and resources can be found in Meier (1988).

While the Common Cause variable does not tap the level of organizational resources or activity of PIRGs, it still provides us with a sense of the extent of support and mobilizable public available to this most important PIRG (McFarland, 1984). I expect that the greater the Common Cause's membership, the lower the ratio.

Finally, to measure more diffuse public interests, I employ a variable as to whether or not the commissioners of the PUC were elected. Such a variable has occasionally been found important in past research (Gormley, 1983, 163–72). I expect that elected PUC commissioners will be sensitive to the concerns of the voters, who prefer a lower ratio.

General economic and social conditions, also representing diffuse interests, might also structure PUC decisions. Three could be crucial here: the percentage of households with service (penetration) (PENET), the percentage of persons below the poverty level (POV), and the percentage of the state's population living in urban areas (URBAN).

In the first case, the lower the state's telephone penetration level, the more the PUC may feel that its universal service mission is incomplete and threatened. Hence, one should expect a lower penetration level to be associated with a smaller rate ratio. But, penetration levels may be low because rates are high. However, the fact that both rates and penetration levels rose in the postdivestiture period lessens the possibility of such an interaction, and studies have found that telephone demand is not very elastic with respect to price (Federal Communications Commission, 1987).

In the second case, the poorer the state's residents, the less likely that they will be able to afford telephone service, and thus, the greater the potential impact of rate increases on subscribership. Therefore, the poorer the state's population, the more the PUC will promote a smaller ratio. However, the inelasticity between demand and price may weaken this potential effect.

Finally, since my concern is with urban rates, we should expect that the larger the urban population, the more the PUC will feel pressure to decrease the rate ratio. In addition, because so many cross-state studies find regional differences, I employ a control variable for SOUTH, defined as the eleven states that joined the confederacy.

Testing the Basic Model

The basic multiple interest model suggests that bureaucrats, politicians, and interests—both private and public—might have impact on telephone rate policies. At this stage of the analysis I assume a linear, additive effects model, as is the case in most existing research, whereby telephone rate policies, the ratio of residential-to-business rates in particular, are incrementally adjusted to conform to the preferences of the several actors trying to exert influence. This incremental adjustment allows the PUC regulators to legitimate their decisions by pointing to the fact that all interested parties with legitimate claims have been heard and responded to. Further, in the process of adjustment, the PUCs build large support coalitions among these interested parties, thereby securing their role in the policy-making subsystem; maintaining their discretion, power, and prestige; and fending off future attacks from the disgruntled.

I use multiple regression to test the impact of bureaucratic, political, and interest group effects on the telephone rate policy. The design, a pooled cross–sectional time series, raises a number of complications, including the possibility of spatial and temporal autocorrelation (Pindyck and Rubinfeld, 1981, 252–61; Stimson, 1985). Diagnostics revealed a potential for both problems in the data set. While less than desirable, I opted for the least squares dummy variable method (LSDV) to help with potential covariance problems. This involved entering into the equations a dummy variable for each state and each year. As Stimson emphasizes, this procedure is not efficient as it eats up many degrees of freedom. Fortunately, my data set is large enough that this poses only a minor problem. More critical in my choice is the fact that both state and time point dummies were found statistically significant predictors of the dependent variable. Error components, generalized least squares (GLS), and ARIMA models are often unable to account for both time and spatial problems simultaneously (Stimson, 1985).

Most critical, however, is that throughout my data set one encounters scattered missing data, which makes it highly difficult, if not impossible to run GLS or ARIMA models. Hence, I had to rely on the LSDV approach, noting its limitations. Still it has been successfully employed in research. For a recent example of this type of technique see Chubb (1988).[12]

Table 3.6 presents full and reduced-form equations of political, bureaucratic, and interest group impacts on the rate ratio.[13] Six variables had impact, all with the correct sign: legislative party control, legislative rule review, whether the PUC is an arm of the executive, Common Cause membership, percentage of the state's population living in poverty, and the number of PUC employees. Significantly, no private interest variable had impact—a finding that strongly undermines the interest group capture theories, at least for this case.

The two legislative variables indicate that when Democratic majorities control the state houses and committees possess strong rule-review provisions, one finds a smaller ratio. Similarly, when the PUC is an arm of the executive branch, the ratio decreases.

While none of the private interest variables had impact, one public interest variable, Common Cause membership, did, indicating that the greater the membership in Common Cause, the more the ratio leans toward residents. And one environmental condition, the state's poverty level, affects the rate ratio—the higher the percentage of people living in poverty the lower the ratio. One bureaucratic variable had impact: the number of PUC employees. As the size of the PUC increases, the ratio increases. I will return to this point, because it has implications for the interest group capture theory.

To better assess the comparative effects of these variables, I convert the regression coefficients into their percentage impact on the rate ratio. (Each 1 percent change equals a .01 change in the ratio's value—remember the ratio can take values from 0.00 to 1.00.)

For instance, each 1 percent increase in Democratic control of the state houses increases the ratio by .67 percent; that is, it increases the burden on business by .67 percent (the ratio changes .0067). This may have considerable cross-state impact because democratic control varies from 20 percent to over 90 percent. Increasing the rule-review power of the legislative committees by one point reduces the ratio .86 percent

Table 3.6

Regression Results of Political, Bureaucratic, and Interest Group Variables on Urban Residential/Business Flat Rates, 1977–85

	FULL MODEL			REDUCED MODEL		
Variable	b	SE	t	b	SE	t
Constant	.67			.50		
BELL	-5.36^{-4}	4.86^{-4}	-1.01	—		
BUSIPCT	-3.06^{-3}	2.61^{-3}	-1.17	—		
CCAUSE	-9.88^{-4}	1.73^{-3}	$-.57$	-1.38^{-3}	5.40^{-4}	-2.56
COMPLEX	-3.27^{-3}	3.13^{-3}	-1.05	—		
CONIN	.01	8.86^{-3}	1.66	—		
ELECTION	.015	.01	1.24	—		
EMPLOY	6.31^{-5}	5.62^{-5}	1.12	1.08^{-4}	3.48^{-5}	3.12
EXARM	$-.02$	.01	-1.53	$-.02$	6.54^{-3}	-2.85
GPARTY	1.46^{-3}	3.32^{-3}	.44	—		
GPOWER	2.94^{-4}	1.54^{-3}	.19	—		
GRASS	.01	.01	1.20	—		
LARM	-1.16^{-3}	.01	$-.11$	—		
LICEN	3.49^{-3}	2.34^{-3}	1.49	—		
LPARTY	-7.13^{-4}	3.29^{-4}	-2.17	-6.71^{-4}	2.17^{-4}	-3.10
LRULE	$-.01$	3.79^{-3}	-2.74	-8.57^{-3}	2.92^{-3}	-2.87
LSAL	4.94^{-3}	6.49^{-3}	.76	—		
PENET	-3.22^{-4}	1.36^{-3}	$-.24$	—		
POV	-6.90^{-3}	2.50^{-3}	-2.76	-4.50^{-3}	1.43^{-3}	-3.15
PROXY	8.24^{-4}	.01	.06	—		
SAFE	-1.74^{-3}	3.66^{-3}	$-.47$	—		

Note: Superscript values are exponents.

Table 3.6 (continued)

	FULL MODEL			REDUCED MODEL		
Variable	b	SE	t	b	SE	t
SOUTH	3.78^{-3}	.01	.32	—		
TIME	5.88^{-3}	8.00^{-3}	.74	—		
URBAN	6.09^{-5}	4.15^{-4}	.15	—		
R^2	.48			.46		
Adj. R^2	.41			.42		
Eq. F	6.34			11.19		
n	280			280		

(.0086 on the ratio). Providing the committees with the maximum in rule power has a lowering effect of 3.4 percent (.034 on the ratio), while converting the PUC into an arm of the executive will lower the ratio 2 percent (.02 on the ratio). Assuming a reasonable maximum legislative seat shift of 10 percent and setting the other variables at their maximum produces a combined effect of almost .13; that is, it may swing the ratio in either direction by 13 percent, a very considerable amount.[14]

How does bureaucratic influence compare with political and interest group influence? Consider a highly mechanical comparison that starkly illustrates the relative impact of bureaucrats and politicians. Each additional PUC employee leads to about a .001 increase in the value of the ratio. To equal the impact of the political variables, a PUC would have to add 130 employees. However, such an increase is highly improbable considering the sizes of the PUCs. The largest PUC has over 900 employees, the smallest 7, but the average has only 118.[15] Just to match the effects of political forces, the average PUC would have to double its size (and probably nearly double its budget to support those new personnel). This is highly unlikely. In fact, from 1977 to 1985, the average PUC added only 18 employees. This represents a strong personnel growth rate, but modest political changes easily overpower it. For instance, a legislative seat swing of only 3 percent in a Democratic direction cancels the entire effect of this growth trend. The point of this exercise is not to suggest that adding employees in large numbers will equalize the impact of bureaucrats and politicians, rather that while a PUC may have impact on the ratio, modest political effects easily overpower it. Still, PUC effects are significant and not to be taken lightly. In later chapters, I explore more deeply the impact of bureaucratic resources.

The results presented here display both continuities and differences from Teske's recent (1990, 1991) analyses. First, one must note that Teske and I study different policy choices. He looked at changes in rate structures and the introduction of intrastate competition. I look at changes in relative rates. Second, he looks at these policies from a purely cross-sectional perspective, while my analysis invokes a time series component, along with the cross sectional one. Third, our model specifications differ in terms of choice of variables.

Still, an overall similarity exists. Teske concludes that institutional factors that relate to the PUCs and legislative control are generally more important predictors of state telecommunications policy choice than interest group factors. Such is the view that my results present, though I unearth gubernatorial effects, something he fails to do because he did not include gubernatorial variables. Not to quibble over variable operationalizations and specifications, what is notable is that given the different analytic approaches and dependent variables, the thrust of the findings converges on the power of institutions, both regulators and politicians, over state telecommunications policy.

Conclusions

PUCs have been concerned with the bypass threat in the postdivestiture era, and consequently should favor policies that reduce the threat. One possible reason that the private interest variables had little direct impact is that the PUCs effectively spoke for them. This may indicate strong responsiveness on the part of the PUCs toward the private interests.

However, what we may be witnessing here is not capture but bureaucrats implementing their own policy preferences, which in this case just happens to coincide with business interests. Such a view is reasonable given that the bulk of current economic theory on telephone pricing evokes fears of bypass. It is reasonable to expect that regulatory bureaucrats would be somewhat conversant with that view and theory.

Further, capture theory predicts that regulated firms and industries are the capturing agents. But I unearthed little evidence deriving from the Bell telephone companies or regulations of possible PUC–telephone company ties. It seems that in this policy arena the PUCs were serving the needs of business users—there is little direct evidence of service to the Bell companies that would cause me to accept a capture argument.

Despite the finding of bureaucratic resources leading to a higher rate ratio, I must caution against acceptance of capture theory. For one thing, executive, legislative, and public interest group factors affected the rate policy as well. And more crucially, the PUCs responded to a diffuse and somewhat inarticulate and inactive group—the impoverished. As poverty rates rose, the relative cost of residential versus business service declined. Adding this finding leads to a perspective according to which bureaucrats try to balance two important competing interests, business and disadvantaged residential users. Such a view is more in line with the interpretation offered here, that regulation is not a neat or simple form of redistribution or protection of either the public or supposedly capturing interests, but rather is a policy type that aims to balance competing interests and claims on public policy.

However, it seems relatively clear that if one removes the political and public interest constraints on the PUCs, they would promulgate policies more favorable to private interests—in this case business users. What checks this tendency is the greater political arena, whereby the public, through elections and other forms of pressure, compete with the better-organized business sector.

The fact that political factors seem so potent compared with bureaucratic ones suggests that political control might be vital for directing the PUCs away from strict service to private interests and more toward accommodating the public. And in so far as political institutions are responsive to diffuse public interests, they might be the only institutionalized mechanisms to ensure that diffuse public interests are served. All of these points suggest a more complex interaction among the political, bureaucratic, and interest group factors than the simple additive effects regression model used. In the next two chapters I model more complex relationships that are based on the notion of conditional influence in the policy-making process.

Notes

1. The following paragraphs are greatly informed by the discussions found in Kahn (1984), Kahn and Shew (1987), MacAvoy and Robinson (1983, 1985),

Temin with Galambos (1987), and Vietor and Davidson (1985).

2. The BOCs, also called "Baby Bells," are NYNEX, Bell South, Ameritech, Bell Atlantic, Pacific Telesis, Southwestern Bell, and US West. Further, the MFJ gave the lucrative Yellow Pages to the Baby Bells to help ensure their profitability and financial solvency during the transition period.

3. The data source for rates is the National Association of Regulatory Commissioners, 1977–85, *Exchange Service Telephone Rates*, Washington, DC: NARUC. The data source for characteristics of the PUCs is National Association of Regulatory Commissioners, 1977–85, *Annual Report on Utility and Carrier Regulation*, Washington, DC: NARUC.

4. Federal charges (the new end-user access fee) and charges for enhanced services (touch-tone, etc.) are not included in this rate. This rate is known in the industry as the rate for POTS (Plain Old Telephone Service).

5. A fourth resource, according to Rourke (1969), is leadership. However, theories of which characteristics about leadership might be important are as yet not well developed and there exists no good way to measure leadership with available data. Hence, while noting the potential importance of this factor, it is not treated explicitly.

6. I also collected budgetary data, which is another type of resource, but across the PUCs there was too much missing data to use it in the analysis.

7. Many PUCs collect user and license fees from those whom they regulate. In some states, those PUCs may keep those monies, to be used to defray administrative costs. In other states, the PUC must remit the revenues to the state (often to the general fund).

8. Another measure that would have been useful is the informational capacity of legislative oversight committees—for instance, staff size on such committees. Such a variable would provide us with some sense of the legislatures' ability to handle information and thus possibly counter bureaucratic monopolization of information. But such data are not available. The legislative salaries and rule-review variables, which measure legislative professionalism and capacity, might indirectly measure this dimension, however.

9. I considered using the Grumm index of legislative professionalism, but it is considerably dated and does not take into account the great strides that some legislatures have made in the ensuing 20 years. However, full reconstruction of that variable was not possible because of the nature of some of its components, which would require a survey of the legislatures.

10. The presence of cross-cutting relationships, here identified as the PUC being an arm of both branches, might alter the relationship between the PUC and the branches, allowing the PUC to play both branches off against each other, selectively running to one branch for protection from the other as circumstances dictate. Interbranch conflict may increase PUC independence from both (Wood, 1988, 214).

11. The body of literature suggesting that a "revolving door" exists is quite large, but the hypothesis is rarely tested. For two tests of it, see Cohen (1986) and Gormley (1979).

12. There are only four data points for 1984 because NARUC did not collect data for that year: it was gearing up for data collection in the divestiture period. Hence, no 1984 dummy was used. I also found that if I drop the insignificant state

and year dummies from the equation, the same results appear.

13. The ns here are smaller because some states did not offer flat-rate service to urban businesses.

14. The formula to calculate this is $(10 * .67) + (.86) + (3.4) + (2.0)$.

15. The average differs from that presented earlier because it is based on those cases that are in the regression equation ($n = 280$), whereas the earlier average was based on all cases in the data set ($n = 459$). Missing data on variables in the regression equation led to this difference. For instance, some states do not offer flat rates to urban businesses.

4

Relative Resources and Public Policy Making

Introduction

The previous chapter began the analysis of the impact of politicians, bureaucrats, and interests groups on telephone policy during the 1977–85 period. However, the underlying model presented there was relatively naive, as it assumed that each actor's influence was independent of the other actors and we can describe policy outcomes as a linear combination of the influence attempts of the several participants in the policy-making process. I challenge that assumption in this chapter. Here I will argue that the policy influence that derives from the resources that each actor possesses is constrained by the resources of other, competing actors. In effect, complex and often subtle interactions among the various participants in the telephone policy subsystem condition how and to what extent each participant can affect regulatory policy outcomes. This theoretical orientation, first presented in the introduction, I call *the theory of relative resources.*

In building the theoretical perspective, I first focus on political versus bureaucratic influence. Then I add interest groups to the model. The theory of relative resources leads to propositions and hypotheses that often run counter to those of other, competing theories—such as interest group capture. Moreover, as I will demonstrate, a test of the relative resources perspective illustrates its superiority over those competing explanations.

The Theory of Relative Resources

Bureaucrats versus Politicians

In a particularly influential work, Francis Rourke (1969) identifies four resources that should increase bureaucratic influence in the policy process. They are: supportive bureaucratic publics (pp. 11–37); bureaucratic skills, including expertise (pp. 39–61); quality leadership (pp. 63 and 76–82); and endowments such as financial and personnel resources (p. 63; also see Meier, 1987, especially chapter 3).[1] In effect, Rourke's discussion suggests that as bureaucratic resources increase, bureaucratic influence over the policy process should also increase. However much Rourke's work has affected our thinking, and it has done so considerably, it is still limited. An example helps illustrate its limitations.

Consider two bureaucratic agencies, the Defense Department (DOD) and the Small Business Administration (SBA). DOD might be the classic highly endowed agency; surely there are few agencies that can equal DOD's level of resources, its professionalism, employee power, and budgetary base. In comparison, SBA is much less well endowed, its staff is smaller and less professionally oriented, and it has a much smaller budget.

A Rourkean perspective would predict that DOD should be more influential in its policy sphere than SBA. However, we may argue that SBA carries more relative influence than DOD. Issue salience, the presence of prestigious committees, and the need for technical expertise may all affect the comparative quality of the politicians overseeing the two agencies. DOD must contend with highly motivated politicians, who not only possess a strong resource base, but who are also keenly interested in the substance of policy. The resource base may derive from the technical nature of many defense decisions (which weapons systems to buy, where to deploy them, how much money to spend on defense), and the potentially conflictual nature of defense policy. Further, the large bite that defense takes out of the budget, the "guns versus butter" trade-offs that appear so often in political rhetoric, and the implications of these factors on public opinion, all impel politicians to try to influence defense policy.

Thus, politicians develop well-staffed legislative oversight committees, containing knowledgeable personnel, while key legislators also become experts in the defense policy area (e.g., Senators Sam Nunn [D–Georgia] and William Cohen [R–Maine] and Representative Les Aspin [D–Wisconsin]). The White House also possesses significant resources, such as the staff of the National Security Adviser, which provides the president with independent and expert defense policy advice.

In contrast, SBA faces legislators who are more concerned with the political implications of policies. Committee oversight staff are less professionalized and the White House rarely is interested in SBA policy. In its policy subsystem, small business policy is neither very contentious nor conflictual. These factors may all lead to high levels of SBA input into policy design—of course with an eye on political benefits to politicians (Arnold, 1979).

Hence, we may suggest that the SBA has more impact on small business policy than DOD has on defense. The simple proposition that "resources equals influence," what we can call *the theory of absolute resources,* which motivated the analysis of chapter 3, fails to appreciate the interaction of bureaucratic and political resources.

Our alternative theory, the theory of relative resources, distinguishes between absolute and relative resources. Figure 4.1 presents a schematic that will help outline the theory. For simplicity's sake, I dichotomize bureaucratic and political resources into high and low, recognizing that these dimensions are continuous. Then I ask, when will bureaucrats or politicians have greater impact over policy?

When bureaucratic resources are high and political resources low, bureaucrats lead in policy influence. This is the cell that the bureaucratic resources or Rourke's perspective explains. In the other high/low cell, politicians dominate. The standard political control models explain this cell best. Examples of this condition can be seen with the federal regulatory commissions, many of which have large tasks but comparatively small staffs, while politicians, especially legislators, have the motivation and wherewithal to participate in and affect commission decisions.

In the upper-left cell, when both politicians and bureaucrats possess reasonably similar and high levels of resources, policy impact is shared. While both have impact, neither would have as much as they could when they possess a resource advantage, and it becomes difficult to predict who directs policy on any particular issue. More likely, we will find bureaucrats winning sometimes and politicians winning other

Figure 4.1 **Resources and Policy Influence: Who has the Greatest Impact?**

| | | Bureaucratic Resources | |
		High	Low
Political Resources	High	Politicians and Bureaucrats Share Influence	Politicians
	Low	Bureaucrats	Interest Groups

times. The DOD example fits into this high/high cell. Critically, the absolute resources perspective can not explain outcomes under these high/high resource conditions. Thus, the relative resources perspective allows us to derive a theoretical expectation that the simpler absolute resources perspective cannot explain.

Still, discussion of the implications of the relative resources theory is incomplete. Focusing exclusively on politicians and bureaucrats does not account for the often strong influence of interest groups. Nor have I as yet offered an explanation of what happens when both politicians and bureaucrats lack resources.

Interest Groups

The theory of relative resources suggests that when interest groups possess a resource advantage over politicians and bureaucrats, interest groups should lead in policy influence. This condition holds only when both politicians and bureaucrats are relatively low in resources, but interests enjoy higher resource levels. The bottom right-hand cell on Figure 4.1 allows for this possibility.

Predictions derived from the relative resources theory contrast with those of the interest group influence theories. The strongest version of interest group influence, capture, suggests that the relative resource discussion is irrelevant (Bernstein, 1955; Stigler, 1971). In all instances, interest groups dominate the policy process and/or its outcomes. Without the mobilization and organization of interests, no public policy will be forthcoming. Thus, even when bureaucrats or politicians possess resources, they are merely the agents of interest groups.

Whereas the interest group perspective predicts ubiquitous interest group influence, the relative resources perspective predicts interest group influence only when interest groups possess a resource advantage over politicians and bureaucrats—that is, when interest groups possess high levels of resources, but politicians and bureaucrats do not. Thus, one finds divergent predictions between the relative resources theory and versions of interest group theory.

Absence of Resources

Our discussion needs to address one more logical possibility. What happens when politicians, bureaucrats, and interest groups all lack substantial resources? When none of the three possesses high levels of resources, none will be able to exert a systematic influence on policy. Under these low-resource conditions, we should not be able to detect a systematic impact of resources on public policy for any of these three actors. Other factors, which may appear to be random or accidental, will determine policy outputs. Among the most likely candidates motivating policy under low-resource conditions are circumstance, events, crises, scandals, and personalities. While one will not be able to determine which factor(s) determine(s) policy under low resource conditions, one can offer an empirical prediction derived from the relative resources theory: The measured resources of the three primary policy actors will exert no detectable influence when held at too low a level. This contrasts sharply with the interest group perspective, which would still predict interest group dominance over policy.[2] And the absolute resources perspective is silent about what happens when all three lack resources.

There exist three competing perspectives on the determinants of policy outcomes: absolute resources, relative resources, and interest group influence. The theories might offer differing expectations, which we may view as critical tests. Table 4.1 lists the competing predictions of the theories. Only the relative resources perspective allows predictions for all possibilities. While this makes it the broadest and most general of the three theories, a comparative test is required to determine which is superior.

Variable Construction

Testing the relative resources theory requires (1) measures of resources for politicians, bureaucrats, and interest groups, (2) measures of their

Table 4.1

Predictions Derived from the Absolute Resources, Relative Resources, and Interest Group Influence Theories

	Resource Level			Theory and Prediction*	
Politicians	Bureau-cracy	Interest Groups	Absolute Resources	Relative Resources	Interest Groups
HIGH	LOW	LOW	Polit.	Polit.	Interests
LOW	HIGH	LOW	Bureau.	Bureau.	Interests
HIGH	HIGH	LOW	no predict.	Pol/Bur. share	Interests
LOW	LOW	HIGH	no predict.	Interests	Interests
LOW	LOW	LOW	no predict.	none has impact	Interests
HIGH**	HIGH	HIGH	no predict.	all share	Interests
HIGH**	LOW	HIGH	no predict.	Pol/IG share	Interests
LOW**	HIGH	HIGH	no predict.	Bur/IG share	Interests

*Prediction is which of the three actors will have the most impact on policy outcomes.
**Not tested due to lack of sufficient case for analysis.

preferences, and (3) other variables whose impact is not predicated on the conditional effects of resources but still might affect policy outcomes.

Resources

To conduct the analysis, I begin by defining high and low political and bureaucratic resources. In denoting the high and low resource cutoff points, I aimed roughly to equalize cases in the high and low categories, while also maintaining variance within each category.[3]

We initially focus on the following four resources: legislative rule-review powers (LRULE), whether or not the PUC is an arm of the executive branch (EXARM), the number of PUC employees (EMPLOY), and Common Cause membership per 10,000 (CCAUSE). I call these the base-resource variables. They represent resources for each of the three hypothesized policy actors, including both the legislative and executive branches.

We begin with these variables as a starting point in defining high and low resource levels because they were found to be significant in the absolute resources–additive effects model presented in chapter 3. This decision provides us with a way to weed through the large number of variables (18—see chapter 3) and variable combinations required for the analysis to follow. After using these variables to define high and low resources levels, the analysis was extended to the other variables. However, analysis revealed that none of them had any statistical impact independent of the impact found for these four base variables. Hence, in the presentation to follow I limit the discussion to these significant variables. This accounts for why private interest group resources are absent here. Table 4.2 details the operation definitions of the final variables used in the analysis.

Specifically, I define high bureaucratic resources as a PUC with over 110 employees. Low bureaucratic resources are defined as a PUC with 110 or fewer employees. High political resources occur when the legislature has two or more rule-review powers (out of four) and the PUC is an arm of the executive branch.

Next, I create two bureaucratic variables, one for each political resource condition. This is done by setting to zero the value for the bureaucratic variable when the political resource condition does not hold. For instance, to create the bureaucratic variable when political resources are high, I assign the scaled values of the bureaucratic variable when political resources are high, otherwise the variable takes on zero values. I label this variable EMPLOY * HIPOLRES (see Table 4.2). Its companion variable, when political resources are low, is created the same way except that now bureaucratic resources takes on scaled values when political resources are low and zero otherwise. This variable is labeled EMPLOY * LOPOLRES. (This process is comparable to creating two dummy variables, one for high political resources, the other for low, and creating two new variables by multiplying the bureaucratic resources variable against each dummy.)

I create the political variables using the same procedure except that now the bureaucratic resources variable sets the variable criteria. Four political variables are created because we had two to begin with, legislative rule review and arm of the executive.

The logic of the analysis is similar to what Wright terms the *conditional effects model* (Wright, 1976). That is, we are comparing the impact of a variable when it belongs to one group or another: Here the grouping refers to the resource level of the competitor.

In this case, then, the relative resources theory predicts that when the conditioning variable is at its low resource state, its complementary variable will affect policy outcomes. However, when the conditioning

Table 4.2

Definitions of Variables Used in the Analysis

BURRES =   A dummy variable that equals 1 when bureaucratic resources are high, zero otherwise.

CCAUSE * HIPOLBURES = COMMON CAUSE MEMBERSHIP PER 10,000 WHEN EITHER POLITICAL OR BUREAUCRATIC RESOURCES ARE HIGH (When either political or bureaucratic resources are low, the variable assumes a zero value.)

CCAUSE * LOPOLBURES = COMMON CAUSE MEMBERSHIP PER 10,000 WHEN EITHER POLITICAL OR BUREAUCRATIC RESOURCES ARE LOW (When either political or bureaucratic resources are high, the variable assumes a zero value.)

EMPLOY * HIPOLRES =   PUC EMPLOYEE LEVELS WHEN POLITICAL RESOURCES ARE HIGH (When political resources are low, the variable assumes a zero value.)

EMPLOY * LOPOLRES =   PUC EMPLOYEE LEVELS WHEN POLITICAL RESOURCES ARE LOW (When political resources are high, the variable assumes a zero value.)

EXARM * HIBURRES =   PUC IS AN ARM OF THE EXECUTIVE WHEN BUREAUCRATIC RESOURCES ARE HIGH (When bureaucratic resources are low, the variable assumes a zero value.)

EXARM * LOBURRES =   PUC IS AN ARM OF THE EXECUTIVE WHEN BUREAUCRATIC RESOURCES ARE HIGH (When bureaucratic resources are high, the variable assumes a zero value.)

LPARTY * HIPOLRES =   LEGISLATIVE PARTY CONTROL WHEN POLITICAL RESOURCES ARE HIGH (When political resources are low, the variable assumes a zero value.)

LPARTY * LOPOLRES =   LEGISLATIVE PARTY CONTROL WHEN POLITICAL RESOURCES ARE LOW (When political resources are high, the variable assumes a zero value.)

LRULE * HIBURRES =   LEGISLATIVE RULE REVIEW POWERS WHEN BUREAUCRATIC RESOURCES ARE HIGH (When bureaucratic resources are low, the variable assumes a zero value.)

LRULE * LOBURRES =   LEGISLATIVE RULE REVIEW POWERS WHEN BUREAUCRATIC RESOURCES ARE HIGH (When bureaucratic resources are high, the variable assumes a zero value.)

Table 4.2 *(continued)*

POLRES =   A dummy variable that equals one when political
                  resources are high, zero otherwise.

variable is high, the impact of the complementary variable is muted.
That is, when political resources are low, bureaucratic impact is hypothesized to surge, but when political resources are high, bureaucratic
impact should wane. Thus, I caution the reader in studying the results
given below. Impacts are associated with the "low resources" variables, not the "high resources" ones, because *low* and *high* designate
the state of the *conditioning variable,* not of the variable hypothesized
to have an effect.

We must also deal with the public interest group variable, CCAUSE.
The relative resources hypothesis suggests that interest groups should
have influence only when the interest has a resource advantage over *both*
politicians and bureaucrats. Thus, I define two new dummy variables, one
for when either political or bureaucratic resources are high
(HIPOLBURRES), and the other for when both are low
(LOPOLBURRES). Then I multiply the Common Cause variable by both
of these new dummies (CCAUSE * HIPOLBURRES, CCAUSE *
LOPOLBURRES), giving us two new public interest group variables.
Again, we expect Common Cause effects on policy outcomes when
both political and bureaucratic resources are low, but when either or
both are high, we should not detect impacts associated with the public
interest group. (As noted above, I used the same procedure on all of the
other political, bureaucratic, and interest group variables, but because
none of the resultant pairs had any significant statistical effects, I do
not discuss them further.)

Preferences

The relative resources theory also suggests that the preferences of
bureaucrats and politicians should affect the magnitude of the rate
ratio. To specify this component of the model, I use two dummy variables, one for high political resources (POLRES) and one for high
bureaucratic resources (BURRES).[4] We can read these dummy variables as shifts in the constant term associated with high and low resources.[5] But like the resource variables created above, these dummies

can cause interpretive confusion unless we keep in mind that the bureaucratic variable tells us about the impact of political preferences and the political dummy tells us about bureaucratic preferences.

Thus, when bureaucratic resources are high, political preferences will be mitigated, but when bureaucratic resources are low, political-preference impacts will surge. And when political resources are high, bureaucratic-preference impacts will temper, but when political resources are low, bureaucratic-preference impacts will rise. Hence, we should see a negative sign associated with the bureaucratic-resources dummy and a positive sign for the political-resources dummy.

Political preferences may also vary with party affiliation. I capture this effect by adding a legislative party control variable (the average percent Democratic of the two chambers). Again, resource levels may affect the impact of preferences on policy outcomes. Following the logic of the resources model, we expect party-related preferences to be felt more strongly when political resources are high rather than low. Thus, I create two new legislative-preference variables, one for high political resources, the other for low political resources, by multiplying the legislative party variable by the high and low political resource dummies (LPARTY * HIPOLRES, LPARTY * LOPOLRES).[6]

Nonmediated Effects

Finally, social and economic conditions can affect the ratio directly; political and bureaucratic resources will not mediate their effects. These conditions can include poverty, urbanization, and telephone penetration levels. Of those that were tried, only the percentage of the state's population living in poverty had any impact (see chapter 3).

Analysis

The relative resources theory must meet two tests before one can accept it. First, it must be internally consistent. Second, it must be more powerful than its competitors. Table 4.3 presents the pooled cross sectional–time series results.

Internal Consistency

We begin by comparing the impact of the resource variables under the high- and low-resource conditions. Consider the political variables,

Table 4.3

Regression Results of Relative Resources on Residential/Business Rates, 1977–85

Variable	b	SE	t
Constant	.56		
LPARTY * LOPOLRES	-1.02^{-3}	3.01^{-4}	-3.37
LPARTY * HIPOLRES	-5.43^{-4}	2.26^{-4}	-2.40
LRULE * LOBURRES	$-.03$	6.29^{0}	-4.48
LRULE * HIBURRES	-9.68^{-3}	6.41^{-3}	-1.51
EXARM * LOBURRES	$-.05$	.02	-2.78
EXARM * HIBURRES	$-.03$	.03	$-.85$
EMPLOY * LOPOLRES	5.71^{-5}	6.75^{-5}	.85
EMPLOY * HIPOLRES	-6.85^{-5}	9.40^{-5}	$-.73$
CCAUSE * LOPOLBURRES	-3.12^{-3}	1.00^{-3}	-3.12
CCAUSE * HIPOLBURRES	2.83^{-3}	1.11^{-3}	2.54
POV	-4.91^{-3}	1.46^{-3}	-3.37
POLRES	.02	.03	.92
BURRES	$-.045$	.02	-2.66
R^2	.51		
Adj. R^2	.46		
Eq. F	9.82		
n	280		

arm of the executive and legislative rule review. As the relative resources theory predicts, both have greater impact when bureaucratic resources are low rather than high. Further, neither is statistically significant when bureaucratic resources are high. However, when bureaucratic resources are low, both are statistically significant and possess the correct sign.

More modest support is found when looking at the impact of political resources on bureaucratic influence. When political resources are low, bureaucratic influence is at best modest. The variable does not reach statistical significance, though its sign is in the correct direction. (If one were to drop this variable from the equation, the R^2 drops a statistically significant amount, indicating that the insignificant t value is due to multicollinearity with other variables.)

However, when political resources are high, the bureaucratic sign reverses. The sign reversal may indicate that when political resources are high, bureaucrats adjust their policy outputs (or policy preferences) in accordance with the preferences of their political principals. This is an unexpected result, but it is not inconsistent with the relative resources model. It indicates that political control may be very effective irrespective of bureaucratic resources when political resources are high. When political resources are low, though, bureaucratic influence over policy outcomes is more consistent with the preferences of bureaucrats. This variable also fails to reach statistical significance, but again, multicollinearity problems associated with the variable cause this statistical insignificance.

Finally, we find supportive evidence when inspecting the impact of Common Cause. The public interest group's influence surges when both political and bureaucratic resources wane. Its sign is correct and the t value is quite strong. However, when resources are high, the sign reverses. It is also statistically significant. Such a finding runs counter to expectations. The relative resources theory would predict an insignificant coefficient, while both the absolute resources and interest group models would predict a negative sign. At this point I have no good explanation for this reversed sign. Later I deal with the impact of Common Cause from the interest group perspective. That later test indicates that perhaps we have encountered a statistical artifact or misspecification in the equation as estimated here.

We can also compare the impact of the "high" and "low" resource variable sets when only one set is included in the equation. That is, I estimated a "low resources" equation. It includes LRULE * LOBURRES, EXARM * LOBURRES, EMPLOY * LOPOLRES, CCAUSE * LOPOLBURRES, plus the LPARTY variables, POV, BURRES and POLRES, and the state and year dummies. I also estimated a "high resources" equation, including LRULE * HIBURRES, EXARM * HIBURRES, EMPLOY * HIPOLRES, CCAUSE * HIPOLBURRES, plus the LPARTY variables, POV, BURRES and POLRES, and the state and year dummies. Recall that since impacts are felt by variables when the grouping variables are low rather than high, we should find that the "low resources" equation is more statistically potent than the "high resources" equation. This is just what we find. The R^2 for the "low" resources equation is .47; the "high" resources R^2 drops to .43. Although seemingly modest, an F test comparison of the two R^2s demonstrates that they are significantly different ($F = 3.62$, which is significant at the .01 level.)

At this initial stage of the analysis, the relative resources theory fares quite well. Two of the comparisons strongly adhere to theoretical predictions (arm of the executive, rule review). A third, PUC employee levels, generally supports expectations, though the results are not as statistically powerful as we would hope. The fourth variable, Common Cause, in part supports the theory, but the reversed sign for the high political-bureaucratic resources is bothersome. In all, considering the bluntness of both the measurement of resources and the categorization of high and low resources, the results are quite supportive of the relative resources theory.

Although not an integral part of the relative resources theory, the results concerning the impact of preferences is also of note. Legislative preferences exert significant influence no matter the level of political resources. In both cases the signs are correct, and the impact is slightly larger when resources are low (a finding somewhat counter to expectations). I reconstructed the legislative party variables, eliminating the executive component from the definition of high resources. Redefining it this way produces essentially the same results.

The dummy variables for high bureaucratic and political resources also provide us with useful information. The bureaucratic dummy variable tells us about the impact of political preferences. Thus, when bureaucratic resources are high, political impacts will be muted; when bureaucratic resources are low, political impacts will surge. Similarly, the political-resources dummy variable tells us about the impact of bureaucratic preferences. We expect, then, a negative sign (a smaller ratio) for the bureaucratic-resources dummy, and a positive sign (a bigger ratio) for the political-resources dummy. This is exactly what we find.

Although it has the correct sign, the political-resources dummy is not statistically significant. Still, the b indicates about a 2 percent shift in the constant. That is, the rate ratio will be depressed about 2 percent. In contrast, the bureaucratic-resources dummy, which captures the impact of political preferences, is much stronger. It is statistically significant and shows a 4.5 percent shift downward in the ratio.

Comparative Power

The second standard that we must address is how powerful the relative resources theory is compared with its competitors.

Absolute Resources

The absolute resources theory suggests that the absolute, not relative, level of resources, determines the impact of actors. This theory was tested with a straight additive effects equation, as I did in chapter 3 (see Table 3.5) when I estimated two such equations, one including all variables for which I collected data, the other using only the significant base resource variables: poverty, legislative party control, and the state and year dummies.

The important comparison here is the R^2. The explained variance for the relative resources model is .51, while the reduced-form additive effects (absolute resources) model shows an R^2 of .46. (I compare these two sets of equations because the relative resources equation includes only combinations of the variables found in the reduced-form additive effects equation.) An F test confirms that the relative resources model is statistically more powerful than the reduced-form absolute resources–additive effects model ($F = 4.22$, which is significant at the .01 level). Clearly, the relative resources specification outperforms the linear, additive absolute resources specification.

Interest Group Influence

The second theoretical competitor is the interest group influence theory. This theory suggests that under any condition, interest groups will have influence over, if not actually determine, policy outcomes. In fact, in one crucial instance the relative resources and interest group approaches diverge: when neither politicians, bureaucrats, nor interest groups have resources, the relative resources theory predicts a random pattern to policy outcomes. In contrast, the interest group approach suggests that even modest levels of interest group resources will suffice and that interest groups will influence policy outcomes.

To compare these competing theories, I partitioned the data into subsets of cases based on varying levels of political, bureaucratic, and interest group resources. The subset definitions are listed on Table 4.2. Then I estimated the same equation for each subset. The equation uses the four base resource variables, plus poverty, legislative party control, and the state and year dummies—the reduced-form equation of Table 4.3. (The high/low resources variables need not be used because the case partitioning produces the same effect and the number of variables and combinations proved too unwieldy to use the estimation technique of Table 4.3.)

Results in Table 4.4 display the regression coefficients and *t* values only for the Common Cause variable, the variable of interest here. Results dramatically support the relative resources theory: no support for the interest group influence theory is uncovered. Specifically, when political resources are high, Common Cause has no impact over this rate policy. However, when political resources are low, Common Cause impact increases, with the correct sign and a strong *t* value. Similarly, when bureaucratic resources are high, Common Cause has no impact, but when bureaucratic resources ebb, again the impact of Common Cause surges, again with the correct sign, but just barely reaching statistical significance at the .05 level. Further, when either politicians or bureaucrats have high resource levels, Common Cause fails to reach statistical significance, but when neither politicians nor bureaucrats have high resource levels, Common Cause impact reaches its peak—both the *b* and the *t* values are stronger than for any subset yet analyzed. Also note that this case subsetting seems to deal effectively with the problem of the reversed sign noted earlier, indicating some kind of misspecification or artifact in the procedure used in Table 4.3.

A crucial test is when none of the three have resources. Results indicate that under these conditions, and contrary to the interest group thesis, Common Cause has no impact on the consumer-to-business ratio. Table 4.5 presents the full equation results for that last condition, when no actor has resources. Not one of the political, bureaucratic, or interest group variables has a strong impact. Only the arm of the executive variable barely surpasses the .10 significance level. By another standard, that the *b* value be twice its standard error, the arm of the executive variable fails to reach statistical significance. What variance is accounted for derives from the state and year dummies, which may be read as the random effects that I suggested might account for policy outcomes under low-resource conditions. (I should note that the healthy R^2 for this equation is a result of those state and year dummies.) All told, this is strong evidence in support of the relative resources perspective, not interest group influence, or its stronger version, interest group capture.

Conclusions

The aim of this chapter is to build and test a theory of public policy making. The theory integrates the literature on political, bureaucratic,

Table 4.4

Impact of Common Cause under Varying Resource Conditions*

Condition	b	t	n
1. High Political Resources	1.68^{-4}	$-.09$	51
2. Low Political Resources	-3.40^{-3}	-3.27	237
3. High Bureaucratic Resources	2.54^{-3}	1.60	115
4. Low Bureaucratic Resources	-1.22^{-3}	-1.84	173
5. Either High Bureaucratic or High Political Resources	-7.05^{-4}	$-.99$	151
6. Both Low Bureaucratic and Low Political Resources	-5.62^{-3}	-4.25	129
7. Low Bureaucratic, Political, and Common Cause Resources	6.68^{-3}	$.41$	88

*All seven equations also control for legislative rule review, legislative party control, arm of the executive, PUC employees, poverty rate, plus the state and year dummies.

and interest group influence through the concept of relative resources. The relative resources theory suggests that before we can assess the impact of an actor on the subsystem, we must take into account the resources other actors possess. In the competition between politicians and bureaucrats for control of policy, resource advantages for either enables them to have greater impact over the policy decision. Further, when both politicians and bureaucrats possess only limited resources, interest groups affect regulatory policy outcomes more strongly. In contrast to views of public-policy decision making that focus exclusively on one branch of government or one type of interest (e.g., interest group capture), the relative resources theory provides not only a broader view that integrates the impact of various actors, but tells us when we should expect one or another actor to dominate.

A statistical test of the theory using telephone rate data proved supportive. Not only did the statistical test show the theory's internal consistency, but comparisons demonstrated the relative resources theory to be more powerful than its major rivals, interest group influence and absolute resources, and this was accomplished even though the

Table 4.5

Impact of Politicians, Bureaucrats, and Interest Groups When None Has High Resource Levels

Variable	b	t
Constant	.47	
Legislative Party	-7.01^{-4}	-1.40
Legislative Rule Review	$-.01$	-1.38
Arm of the Executive	$-.04$	-1.84
PUC Employees	1.27^{-4}	.36
Common Cause	6.68^{-3}	.41
Poverty	-3.15^{-3}	$-.64$
R^2/Adj. R^2	.65/.58*	
F/n	8.93/88	

* R^2s and adjusted R^2s of this size when the listed variables show no effects are due to the inclusion of the state and year dummy control variables that are used in this and all other equations.

measurement of resources and the construction of the relative resources variables were crude at best.

Theoretically, relative resources provides us with a statistically powerful but also rich and subtle explanation of policy making. It is also a theory that incorporates only modest assumptions, the key one being that resource impacts on the policy making of one actor depend on the resources of the competing actors. The next chapter raises another conditional resources issue relating to the efficiency of the translation of resources: How well do electoral institutions translate public preferences into policies?

Notes

1. Note, however, that Meier allows for an interactive relationship between bureaucrats and politicians (1987, 43–45), although he does not develop the point.
2. The interest group theory would suggest that all that is required to promote policy in accord with the preferences of the interest is that it be organized. Thus, the mere fact of organization is enough of an asset or a resource to result in

favorable policies for the interest group.

3. Considerable experimentation was conducted to determine reasonable cut-off points as theory was unable to guide us. We really have no theory that tells us what quantity a resource must take before it reaches a threshold of being substantial. Initial experimentation included the variables that were subsequently dropped from the analysis. However, I found that elaborating on the definition of high and low resources by adding conditions from these other variables was generally redundant or created problems of loading too many cases into one group or the other. Hence, the somewhat simpler definitions were found to be optimal for present purposes.

4. A variable for both high political and bureaucratic resources could not be entered into the equation because it is a linear combination of the other two dummy variables.

5. In the conditional effects model, Wright (1976) also suggests that these dummy "intercepts" are necessary to specify the equation fully and to determine the effect of grouping cases.

6. A similar procedure found no impact for the gubernatorial party variable.

5

Direct Democracy and Public Policy Outcomes: The Impact of Elections on Bureaucratic Decision Making (Or Should We Elect Our Regulators?)

Introduction

Under what conditions will elections promote policies that the general public prefers as opposed to those of a special interest? Casual observers assume that elections motivate policy toward public preferences, but little research directly bears on that question. I argue below that elections can promote such policies, but only under certain conditions. To do so, elections must not only sensitize decision makers to public preferences, but the institution in which decision makers hold positions must have the capability to convert those preferences into policies. This perspective differs from the more commonly held view that election itself is *necessary and sufficient* to produce policies congruent with public preferences. I will present the theoretical framework and test it on the telephone rate policies discussed throughout.

A Conditional Effects Perspective on Electoral Impacts

We can conceive of a policy continuum where public preferences (defined as majority preferences) anchor one pole and the preferences of a special interest anchor the other. For elections to affect policy outcomes, policy conflict between the public (majority) and a special interest must exist.

By definition, if no majority preference exists, we cannot unambiguously identify a publicly preferred outcome. Several other conditions are theoretically uninteresting or unlikely. For instance, if either the special interest or the public does not have a policy preference, but the other one does, it is hard to imagine policy makers deciding with the disinterested party. And if neither the public nor any special interest has a preference or is assumed to have a policy preference, I cannot imagine policy even being forthcoming.

Without such conflict, we cannot detect whether the presence of elections moves policy towards the public's position or away from the special interest's. Thus, discernible electoral impacts are not ubiquitous but exist only for the class of issues over which public and special interest policy preferences diverge.

Such policy differences between the public and special interests are neither uncommon nor substantively unimportant (Denzau and Munger, 1986). The theory of interest group capture often conceptualizes policy choices this way (Mitnick, 1980), and studies of regulatory policies frequently juxtapose special interests (sometimes called concentrated interests) against the public (sometimes called diffuse interests) (Wilson, 1980). Given these situations, will elections motivate policy toward the public end of the continuum?

Figure 5.1 presents a policy space where only two of four possible quadrants can be filled at any one time. Consider when elections are neither *necessary nor sufficient* to produce policies that accord with public preferences (cells 1 and 2).

This view is rare among scholars and more casual observers, but we can garner some support for it in the literature. For instance, Bunce (1981) detects policy responsiveness in countries that do not elect their leaders and Meier (1987) finds that bureaucrats may hold policy views quite close to the mass public's. Also, the theory of representative bureaucracy suggests that the bureaucracy as a whole may be more representative of the public than the elected branches (Krislov and Rosenbloom, 1981). Thus, institutions other than electorally based ones may promote public preferences and sometimes may even surpass elected bodies at promoting those preferences.

Consider when elections are *necessary and sufficient* to produce policies that the public prefers (cells 1 and 4)—probably the most

Figure 5.1 **Typology of Conditional Electoral Effects**

		Elections	
		Present	Absent
Do Policy Outcomes Correspond with Public Preferences?	Yes	1	2
	No	3	4

widely held and classic view of the virtues (impacts) of elections. Little supportive evidence exists, and what does is inconclusive. For instance, Nagel (1973) detects policy differences between elected and appointed state judges, but Dubois (1980) does not. Similarly, studies of the state public utility commissions, where one-fourth of the states elect their regulators, also show contradictory findings. Some find that elected PUCs produce policies more beneficial to consumers than appointed PUCs (Mann and Primeaux, 1983a, 1983b; Pelsoci, 1979), but others uncover no difference between elected and appointed PUCs (Costello, 1984; Gormley, 1983; Hagerman and Ratchford, 1978; Harris and Navarro, 1983). Hence, even this most popular view is not unquestionably supported.

Finally, consider when elections may or may not affect the implementation of the public's preferences (cells 1 and 3). Strong support for this perspective exists. Kuklinski (1978) notes differences in the relative policy representativeness of California representatives and senators. The former more closely correspond to constituency public opinion than the latter, presumably because representatives' terms of office are shorter, and shorter terms enhance the incentives for representatives to respond to public opinion. Similarly, senatorial correspondence with constituency opinion increases as election nears (Kuklinski, 1978, 174), a finding repeated at the U.S. Senate level (Bernstein, 1988; Elling, 1982; Thomas, 1985; and Wright and Berkman, 1986, 1988).

There breathes a debate over the direction of the shift, whether it is toward a moderate or a strategic position. See especially Bernstein (1988) and Wright and Berkman (1988) on this issue. Further, the existence of such a cycle is also debated. Dougan and Munger (1989) do not find a cycle, but still argue that length of term may be important, a position that contrasts sharply with those studies mentioned above, all of which discern a cycle. Thus, the mere fact of election may not be enough to forge a correspondence between the elected and the public. Rather, certain conditions must exist for this to occur. What are those conditions? I focus on conditions that affect the nature and structure of decision makers' incentives and the capability of decision-making institutions to convert public preferences into policies. The design of electoral arrangements and the degree of public mobilization should affect incentives, while institutional resources should affect preference conversion and policy implementation.

Specifying the Conditions for Electoral Impact

Incentives: Electoral Arrangements

Electoral systems can be designed to facilitate or impede incumbent reelection. When easy reelection is impeded, concern with public preferences among officeholders might increase. This should result in policies that better accord with public preferences than if victory were assured.

Short terms, at-large elections, and district competition may all increase election-day vulnerability, thereby amplifying the incentives of elected decision makers to respond to public preferences. While these do not encompass all aspects of electoral systems, they are among the most obvious. If they fail to produce the hypothesized effect, it is unlikely that other less obvious electoral characteristics will.

I also attempted to look at the timing of the election for the PUCs, following Kuklinski (1978), but timing is more appropriate when looking at individual politicians. As all but one PUC used staggered elections, PUC elections occur almost every year or two. Similarly, nonpartisan elections and the size of the elected body may affect responsiveness, but all of the elected PUCs use partisan elections and there is little variation in size of the PUCs. Finally, concurrent elections might be more likely than staggered ones to promote respon–2siveness, but only one state, Mississippi, elected its commissioners concurrently. Including a variable for concurrent versus staggered elections would be the same as adding a dummy variable for Mississippi.

Length of Term

Length of term may affect the visibility and public memory of past decisions (Dougan and Munger, 1989, 124). Representatives might believe that the public can recall their decisions when terms are short rather than long. Long terms allow older decisions to fade from public consciousness. Moreover, longer terms provide decision makers with more opportunities to correct past "incorrect" decisions. Thus, elected bodies where members hold longer tenures may possess less of an incentive to produce policies that the public prefers than bodies offering shorter terms of office.

Empirical evidence supports this proposition (e.g., Kuklinski's [1978] California study cited above; also Amacher and Boyes, 1978). I hypothesize, then, that an elected body with shorter terms of office will promulgate policies that better reflect public preferences than a body with longer terms.

District versus At-Large Election

Size of constituency can also affect policy outcomes. Generally, the public feels that offices representing larger numbers of people are more important than offices representing smaller aggregates. Thus, public concern and motivation to vote increases as does size of constituency. Even modest increases in voter turnout will increase decision makers' incentives to attend to public concerns. Hence, we are −2likely to find that the policies produced by at-large systems are more consistent with majority public preferences than are district-based systems.

The literature suggests that this is the case. Special interests (sometimes called minorities) seem to hold greater sway in district (ward) than at-large systems. Engstrom and McDonald (1981), Robinson and Dye (1978), and Vedlitz and Johnson (1982) all find greater representation of minorities in ward (district) than in at-large cities. Mladenka (1989) finds higher levels of black government employment in ward than in at-large cities, and Lineberry and Fowler (1967) note some policy differences between at-large and ward cities. While these studies do not directly address the question of public versus special-interest preferences, they are nonetheless suggestive.

Competitiveness

While it is more difficult to manipulate the competitive environment than term length or district boundaries (though gerrymandering may be one device to allow the manipulation of district competitiveness), competition nonetheless has great implications for a decision-making body's incentives. Electoral institutions in competitive environments often witness considerable member turnover, mostly due to electoral defeat, and politicians in competitive atmospheres may be highly sensitive to public preferences. Fearing electoral defeat, they may compel their institution to produce policies that serve the larger class of voters, that is, accord with majority public preferences. Thus, competition may drive elected bodies to pursue policies that the public prefers.

A huge literature dating back to V. O. Key's (1949) *Southern Politics* tests variants of this hypothesis. While not all findings support the competitiveness–public policy linkage, the bulk of the research suggests such a relationship.

The literature is too large to be cited fully here. Early studies tended to find competition influencing public policy outcomes (cf. Dawson and Robinson, 1963). A round of revisionist findings challenged the earlier ones, arguing that economic factors, not party competition, had greater impact on policy outcomes (Hofferbert, 1966, and Dye, 1966). Recently, scholars have begun to specify the relationship between competition and policy outcomes more sensitively, finding that under proper conditions, competition indeed affects policy outcomes (cf. Carmines, 1974; Plotnick and Winters, 1985; Sharkansky and Hofferbert, 1969). The last electoral arrangements hypothesis suggests that as competition increases, so does the likelihood that the decision-making body will produce policies that accord with public preferences.

Incentives: Public Mobilization

Issues that mobilize the public or are perceived as mobilizing can provide decision makers with another incentive to produce policies that the public prefers. Actual or perceived mobilization may affect policy outcomes through several routes. Mobilization may furnish decision-making bodies with information about public preferences. Articulation of demands often attends mobilization (Verba and Nie, 1972). Also, public mobilization may supply decision makers with a rationale to pursue those policies that the public prefers at the expense of those that special interests favor. Fearing election-day public reprisals, decision makers "explain their vote" (Kingdon, 1974) to special interests, arguing that if they were to stay in office (and perhaps serve special interests in the future) they had to side with the public. Such a defense may effectively ward off potential attacks from special interests who understand that over the long haul decision makers will be attentive to them. Finally, decisions makers may fear that if they side with special interests over the public on a potentially mobilizing issue, the attendant surge in turnout will be overwhelmingly composed of voters motivated to cast their ballots against the offending representatives. Hence, to stem election-day reprisals or fear of them, decision makers may collectively produce those policies that resonate with public preferences.

Conversely, lack of public mobilization permits the decision-making body greater latitude in deciding policy directions and outcomes, as well as the opportunity to more attentively serve special interests. Thus, when the public is mobilized, is perceived to be mobilized, or is perceived to be potentially capable of being mobilized, decision—1making bodies will be more likely to produce policies that the public prefers.

Institutional Resources

The elected body must possess the resources to identify public preferences and implement them into public policies. For instance, Carmines (1974) argues that before a legislature can respond to public opinion it must possess the necessary institutional resources to assess public preferences and convert those preferences into public policies—what he calls *legislative professionalism* (cf. also Nice and Cohen, 1979). Students of bureaucracy also argue that bureaucratic influence in the policy-making process covaries with institutional resources (Berry, 1979; Gormley, 1983; Meier, 1987; Rourke, 1969).

Bureaucratic resources have a two-pronged impact on policy production. Resources enhance the bureaucracy's ability to monitor and discern public preferences, while also providing greater influence over the actual implementation process. Hence, we must distinguish between the desire to produce policies that the public wants and actually doing so (Eulau and Karps, 1978; Pitkin, 1967). While decision makers may desire to produce policies compatible with public wishes, without the requisite institutional resources at their disposal they may not be able to do so.

Summary

Elections will affect public policy only under certain conditions—when incumbents feel insecure in office; when the public is mobilized, perceived as mobilized, or perceived as capable of mobilization; and when the decision-making body possesses the requisite institutional resource base. While each condition should heighten electoral impact, the conditional effects perspective suggests an interaction among these factors. Thus, the greatest electoral impact will be felt when politicians feel electorally insecure, when they also face a mobilized public, and also when their institution enjoys measurable resources.

Data and Design

The policy ratio variable is especially suited to these electoral concerns. It directly evokes the conflict between residents (the mass public) and business (a special interest) required to analyze electoral effects. Moreover, it is substantively and politically meaningful. Clearly, residents prefer low rates relative to business, and naturally business prefers the reverse. Much debate in the wake of divestiture centered around how much different customer classes should pay. Soaking the rich (here defined as business) was one policy option that pro-consumer advocates sought. Furthermore, PUC regulators should have no trouble estimating and/or anticipating either the public's or business's policy preferences, and this should be true even if the public failed to articulate a clear policy position.

Ideally, the residential public prefers a rate ratio that approaches zero (the absolute minimum), free service. Under that condition, business users wholly subsidize residents. Business, in contrast, wants to limit or eliminate any subsidy to residential users, preferring rate parity (a ratio of 1.0).

While business, like residents, would like to be subsidized, nowhere in my reading could I find the business sector publicly espousing such a position. Historically, businesses pay more for telephone service than residents. The inertia of history constrains the available policy options to the business community. This keeps the rate ratio between 0.0 and 1.0.

Model estimation employs multiple regression using the least squares dummy variable approach (LSDV) (Stimson, 1985). Dummy variables representing each year and state were entered into the equation to correct for any spatial and/or autocorrelation problems that pooled cross sectional–time series designs would pose (for a recent application see Chubb, 1985).

For the LSDV estimation, I entered one dummy variable for each state (48) and year (9) into the equation. However, if we drop from the final estimations any of the dummies not found to be statistically significant the results remain the same with only trivial shifts in the size of the coefficients of the significant variables. The significant dummy variables are: 1981, 1982, 1983, Arkansas, Colorado, Idaho, Indiana, Minnesota, Mississippi, Missouri, Nevada, Oregon, South Dakota, and Washington.

Finally, as the telephone regulatory environment is complex, and several other actors may influence PUC rate making, we cannot simply compare the rate ratio for states that elect and appoint their regulators. Analysis in chapter 3 revealed six variables with a statistically significant impact on the ratio:

1. the average percentage of Democrats in the two legislative chambers (LPARTY),
2. a measure of legislative committee rule review (LRULE),
3. whether or not the PUC is an arm of the executive branch (EXARM),
4. the number of PUC employees (EMPLOY),
5. the number of Common Cause members per 10,000 (CCAUSE), and
6. the state's poverty level (POV).

These variables are employed in each equation as controls. They also provide a baseline against which to assess electoral effects (see Table 3.6).

Analysis

If elections affect the policy ratio, we should witness shifts in the ratio in a direction favorable to residents (toward 0.0). That is, we should focus on the marginal policy shifts associated with elections, recognizing that other factors also have impact. Thus, analysis will concentrate on the regression coefficients of the electoral and conditional variables, as well as improvement in model performance when those variables are added to the baseline model.

A Preliminary Assessment: Do Elections Matter?

We first compare equation performance including and excluding the election dummy variable. If election itself affects policy outcomes, the election dummy sign should be negative and the ratio should decrease—that is, residential rates relative to business rates should decrease. If it has no significant impact, election is either insufficient to produce hypothesized effects or its impact is conditional. Table 5.1 presents the results.

The election dummy has little impact. The equation's explained variance does not budge (baseline $R^2 = .46$, election dummy addition $R^2 = .46$). Comparison of the adjusted R^2s, which controls for the number of variables in the equation, also shows no improvement in model performance. Moreover, the unstandardized regression coefficient b for the election dummy fails to reach statistical significance by any conventional criterion, even though it possesses the correct sign. If analysis were to stop here, we would conclude that elections have no impact on this policy. However, electoral effects, as demonstrated below, are conditional.

Electoral Arrangements and Policy Responsiveness

The next equation adds to the baseline model variables specifying electoral arrangements: a dummy variable for at-large elections (ATLARGE), PUC commissioners' length of term in years (LENGTH), and the level of party competition for states that elect their PUC commissioners (PARTYC), using the standard index of party competition (Bibby, 1983, 66) to measure the competitive environment. A better measure of competition would use the results of the PUC elections themselves, but such data were not available. Thus, I use the standard measure as a surrogate, arguing that competitiveness is a system characteristic, and should also affect PUC contests.

I rescaled the competition index so that higher values equal higher levels of competition, which removes the party direction component. The rescaling formula is: |Party Competition Score - .5|. All variables take on zero values when the PUC is not elected. Party competition and at-large status should be negative, and length of term positive.

Table 5.1

Comparison of Election and Electoral Arrangements Effects on Residential/Business Rate Ratio

	ELECTION DUMMY			ELECTORAL ARRANGEMENTS		
Variable	b	SE	t	b	SE	t
Constant	.50			.52		
LPARTY	$-.70^{-3}$	$.23^{-3}$	-3.09	$-.95^{-3}$	$.25^{-3}$	-3.79
LRULE	$-.81^{-2}$	$.30^{-2}$	-2.75	$-.84^{-2}$	$.30^{-2}$	-2.86
EXARM	$-.02$	$.66^{-2}$	-2.87	$-.02$	$.69^{-2}$	-3.65
CCAUSE	$-.14^{-2}$	$.55^{-3}$	-2.59	$-.12^{-2}$	$.54^{-3}$	-2.30
EMPLOY	$.10^{-3}$	$.35^{-4}$	3.13	$.13^{-3}$	$.35^{-4}$	3.60
POV	$-.41^{-2}$	$.17^{-2}$	-2.42	$-.41^{-2}$	$.17^{-2}$	-2.43
ELECTION	$-.36^{-2}$	$.75^{-2}$	$-.48$	*		
ATLARGE	*			$-.02$	$.01$	-1.97
LENGTH	*			$.87^{-2}$	$.34^{-2}$	2.57
COMPET	*			$-.13$	$.05$	-2.72
R^2	.46			.48		
Adj. R^2	.42			.43		
n	280			280		
F	10.64			10.26		

*Not in the equation.

These electoral arrangements improve model performance. The R^2 is 2 percent higher than the baseline's (baseline $R^2 = .46$; electoral arrangement model $R^2 = .48$), which an F test determines is a statistically significant increase. The F test compares the R^2s of the baseline and the electoral arrangements equations. The formula is:

$$F_{q,n-k} = \frac{(R^2_e - R^2_b)/q}{(1 - R^2_e)/n - k}$$

where
   q = number of electoral arrangements variables
   n = number of cases
   k = number of variables in the baseline equation
   R^2_e = explained variance for the electoral arrangements equation
   R^2_b = explained variance for the baseline equation.

This formula is adapted from the procedure to compare restricted and unrestricted regression equations (Pindyck and Rubinfeld, 1981, 116–26). The F is 3.50, which is significant at the .01 level (the .01 significance level is 3.4, the .05 level is 2.4). Comparison of the adjusted R^2s also reveals a significant impact. Moreover, the regression coefficients, which present information on direction of impact, support and refine this interpretation. All variables have significant impact in the correct direction. Still, results are modest statistically, and the conditional effects perspective suggests strong interaction effects among electoral arrangements, public mobilization, and bureaucratic resources.

Interaction among Electoral Conditions

Interaction between Electoral Arrangements and Mobilization

The time series component of the data set allows a strong test of the mobilization effects hypothesis. The divestiture of AT&T interrupted the time period. (Divestiture was announced in 1982 and fully implemented in 1984.) Prior to divestiture, the public was rather quiescent and unconcerned about telephone rates. Rates had fallen steeply since the end of Second World War and telephone service was reliable and affordable.

Divestiture changed all of this. Telephone rates began to rise, and the burden of costs began to shift more and more onto consumers. The host of new long distance companies created confusion over billing and what company to select. There was also confusion over who was responsible for repair and maintenance. Most significantly, public debate, often of a demagogic sort, raised fears of steeply spiraling future prices.

Consequently, public concern and interest crested in the wake of divestiture. Harris surveys conducted in November 1984 (survey no. 1247) and February 1986 (survey no. 1255) show that the public feeling was that divestiture was a bad idea.

The exact wording of the survey's questions and the results are as follows:

> *1984*—It's been nearly a year since the Bell system was broken up. As you look back on it, do you think it was a good idea or a bad idea for the Bell system to be broken up?

THE IMPACT OF ELECTIONS 141

1986—It has been just over two years since the Bell system was broken up. As you look back on it, do you think it was a good idea or a bad idea for the Bell system to be broken up?

	1984	1986
	%	%
Good idea	25	26
Bad idea	64	63
Not sure	11	11

In December 1988, *The Washington Post* reported poll results indicating that while the public still viewed divestiture as having been a bad idea, antagonisms had moderated. However, not having exact question-wordings from the *Post* report, we have no way to determine how comparable their results are with the Harris results. In any event, the *Post* found that 39 percent of respondents viewed the breakup as "a bad idea," 31 percent as "a good idea," and 30 percent had no opinion (*Washington Post Weekly Edition*, 9 January 1989, 6–7.)

Similarly, the 1984 Harris survey respondents felt that business benefited more from divestiture than residents. The exact question and results from the Harris survey are as follows:

Since the breakup of the telephone system, who do you think has benefited the most on (SERVICE)(COST)—residential customers or business users of the telephone system?

	Service	Cost
	%	%
Residential customers	11	17
Business users	65	66
Neither (volunteered)	6	4
Both (volunteered)	1	—
Not sure	17	3

And the 1986 Harris survey revealed that by a significant margin, consumers did not feel that their long distance bills had declined, as proponents of divestiture predicted. The question and figures are as follows:

When AT&T was broken up, it was claimed that long distance rates would go down over a period of time. Over the past two years, have your long distance rates gone down, stayed the same, or gone up?

	%
Gone down	13
Stayed the same	41
Gone up	27

Thus, there exists strong evidence of public cynicism and dislike for divestiture. Such an atmosphere should lead PUC commissioners to perceive at least the potential for public mobilization. Other data suggest both increased public attention and mobilization.

One can indirectly gauge increasing public attention absent survey data by inspecting the major mass media news reports. Public interest ranks among the many factors on which journalists rely when selecting items to cover. Using the Vanderbilt Television News and Abstracts, I counted the number of stories aired on all three networks on telephone policy from 1977 through 1985. An average of 5.2 stories were aired between 1977 and 1981. During the postdivestiture years (1982–85) the average jumps to 29.5. The actual figures for each year are as follows: 1977—9; 1978—5; 1979—2; 1980—3; 1981—7; 1982—13; 1983—40; 1984—44; 1985—21. This does not include the 33 stories on the strike against AT&T in 1983. Although the number of stories is small in any year, this represents explosive growth in news coverage, and presumably public attention.

Data on citizen complaints to the PUCs indicate increased public activity concerning telephone regulatory policy. Many of the PUCs annually report levels of citizen complaints against regulated utilities, which we may take as an indicator of public activation. We should, however, use these data cautiously, as many states do not report complaint levels.

Thirty-two states reported reliable and usable data. We can see the increased rates of complaints by comparing average annual levels of complaints for 1977–80 and 1984–85. Overall, complaints increased by 68.8 percent. Nineteen states (59 percent) registered complaint increases: eight (25 percent) noted increases greater than 40 percent; only two (6 percent) saw declines at that level. It appears, then, that the average PUC experienced increased levels of citizen complaints against telephone companies, some of which may be attributable to divestiture and its impact on consumers.

Thus, it seems reasonable to argue that the public mobilized in reaction to divestiture or was ready to be mobilized. At least, PUC regulators should have perceived the potential for public mobilization, and if the hypothesis is correct, after divestiture, election effects should increase as true mobilization rose and/or regulators responded to anticipated mobilization. To test this, I bisected the data into the years prior to (1977–81) and after (1982–85) divestiture's announcement. Table 5.2 presents the results.

In the predivestiture period neither the election dummy nor electoral arrangements adds to the explanatory power of the baseline model. However, matters change during the post-divestiture period. While the election dummy equation still shows no improvement over the baseline, the electoral arrangements equation does, improving the R^2 by 3 percent.

An F test indicates that the improvement is not significant ($F = 2.13$), but if we drop the insignificant length of term variable from the equation, the R^2 remains the same, and the F improves to 3.19, which is significant at the .05 level.

The regression coefficients reveal the interaction of electoral arrangements and public mobilization. While two of the electoral arrangement variables are statistically significant in the postdivestiture period (party competition, at-large), none are significant before its announcement. Cautious comparison of the b's demonstrates that in each case the electoral arrangements variables are larger in the postdivestiture than predivestiture period, suggesting the importance of the interaction effect.[1] This interpretation is bolstered by the fact that the election dummy equation does not differ across the two periods. In both equations the election dummy is statistically insignificant. As expected, interactions between electoral arrangements and mobilization enhance electoral impacts.

Interaction between Electoral Arrangements and PUC Resources

To test the electoral arrangements–bureaucratic resources interaction, I now bisect the data into high and low bureaucratic resources, using the mean value of PUC employee levels—the measure of bureaucratic resources—as the partitioner.

Some might question the use of employee levels, asking *why not create a percapitized measure of employee size?* Basically, because most PUCs are small. The mean is 118 and the largest, California,

Table 5.2

Interaction of Electoral Arrangements and Public Mobilization

| | Public Mobilization | | | | | |
| | Low (1977–81) | | | High (1982–85) | | |
Variable	b	SE	t	b	SE	t
Election Dummy Equation						
Election Dummy	.003	.01	.33	−.02	.01	−1.66
R^2	.46			.54		
Adj. R^2	.40			.44		
F	7.33			5.39		
Electoral Arrangements Equation						
Party Competition	−.09	.07	−1.33	−.14	.07	−2.05
At–Large	−.007	.02	−.45	−.03	.02	−2.03
Length of Term	.006	.005	1.38	.008	.005	1.71
R^2	.47			.56		
Adj. R^2	.40			.45		
F	6.72			5.17		
Baseline Equation						
R^2	.46			.53		
Adj. R^2	.40			.43		
F	7.80			5.43		
n	173			107		

Note: Baseline equation variables are listed in text. They are included in each equation. Only results for the electoral variables are presented.

barely tops 1,000. As a percentage of the population, PUC employment levels are so small as to be meaningless. Table 5.3 presents results of this analysis.

When bureaucratic resources are low, the election dummy equation adds a mere 1 percent to the R^2, a statistically insignificant increment, as the F value of .437 demonstrates. However, the electoral arrangements model significantly improves over the baseline boosting the R^2 by 5 percent.

Table 5.3

Interaction of Electoral Arrangements and Bureaucratic Resources

	Bureaucratic Resources					
	Low			High		
Variable	b	SE	t	b	SE	t
Election Dummy Equation						
Election Dummy	.01	.01	1.09	−.02	.01	−1.32
R^2	.52			.50		
Adj. R^2	.46			.42		
F	9.84			6.89		
Electoral Arrangements Equation						
Party Competition	−.19	.06	−3.01	−.39	.13	−2.99
At–Large	.02	.01	1.28	−.13	.03	−4.00
Length of Term	.01	.004	2.52	.03	.01	3.08
R^2	.56			.58		
Adj. R^2	.51			.51		
F	10.43			8.30		
Baseline Equation						
R^2	.51			.49		
Adj. R^2	.46			.42		
F	10.37			7.27		
n	175			105		

Note: Baseline equation variables are listed in text. They are included in each equation. Only results for the electoral variables are presented.

This improvement pales when compared to the high-bureaucratic-resources equations. Now electoral arrangements enlarge the R^2 by 9 percent over the baseline, while the election dummy evinces no significant impact. An F test demonstrates that the R^2 improvement for the high resources equation is greater than that for the low-resources equation.

Inspection of the regression coefficients also provides supportive evidence. The election dummy variable remains insignificant in both equations. In contrast, while party competition and length of term are significant for low resources, all three electoral arrangements reach statistical significance for the high-resources case.

Again, one can cautiously compare the b's. The party competition b is over twice as large for high resources than it is for low resources. Similarly, the b for length of term is about three times greater for high resources than for low resources. The at-large variable is over six times larger for the high-resources equation than for the low-resources equation. Bureaucratic resources mightily affect the impact of electoral arrangements, as the conditional-effects perspective predicts. Still, a complete theory suggests a more complex interaction pattern involving all three conditions. The next section presents the evidence.

Election, Mobilization, and Resource Interactions

To test the more complex relationships among the three conditions, I divided the data into four subsets: (1) low bureaucratic resources–low mobilization: (2) high bureaucratic resources–low mobilization, (3) low bureaucratic resources–high mobilization; and (4) high bureaucratic resources–high mobilization, with the high and low designations defined as above. If the theory is correct, the convergence of the three conditions should produce the strongest impacts. Table 5.4 presents the results.

Compare the R^2's: The low/low electoral arrangements equation improves on the baseline R^2 by 5 percent, by 5 percent for the low resources–high mobilization equation, and by 6 percent for the high resources–low mobilization equation, while the election dummy shows no impact for any of these three cases. However, the high/high results dwarf these findings.

The electoral arrangements variables add 20 percent to the R^2 over the high/high baseline equation, the largest increment yet, and the adjusted R^2 shows an improvement of 25 percent. The F for the unadjusted R^2 is 16.02 and for the adjusted R^2 is 14.36. Both are easily significant at the .01 level.

A strong effect for the election dummy is also detected in the high/high category: the election dummy boosts the R^2 a statistically significant 14 percent. Yet the electoral arrangements equation beats this by another 6 percent. The F is 4.65 and is significant at the .01

Table 5.4

Complex Interactions among Electoral Arrangements, Bureaucratic Resources, and Public Mobilization

	Low Bureaucratic Resources					
	Low Mobilization			High Mobilization		
Variable	b	SE	t	b	SE	t
Election Dummy Equation						
Election Dummy	.014	.014	.95	−.0006	.02	−.04
R^2 /Adj.R^2/ F	.52	.45	6.88	.64	.51	5.18
Electoral Arrangements Equation						
Party Competition	−.20	.08	−2.47	−.19	.11	−1.80
At–Large	.02	.02	1.15	.03	.02	1.20
Length of Term	.01	.005	2.00	.008	.007	1.22
R^2 /Adj.R^2 /F	.57	.49	7.33	.69	.56	5.47
Baseline Equation						
R^2 /Adj.R^2 /F	.52	.45	7.32	.64	.53	5.64
n	111			64		

	High Bureaucratic Resources					
	Low Mobilization			High Mobilization		
Variable	b	SE	t	b	SE	t
Election Dummy Equation						
Election Dummy	−.008	.02	−.51	−.07	.02	−4.52
R^2 /Adj.R^2 /F	.47	.36	4.11	.79	.71	10.45
Electoral Arrangements Equation						
Party Competition	.06	.05	1.10	−.29	.09	−3.19
At–Large	−.05	.02	−2.54	−.07	.02	−2.99
Length of Term	*			.01	.008	1.44
R^2 /Adj.R^2 /F	.53	.42	4.67	.85	.79	12.81

Table 5.4 *(continued)*

	High Bureaucratic Resources					
	Low Mobilization			High Mobilization		
	b	SE	*t*	*b*	SE	*t*
Baseline Equation						
R^2 /Adj.R^2 /F	.47	.37	4.56	.65	.54	5.89
n	62			43		

*Not in the equation (variable tolerance too low).
Note: Baseline equation variables are listed in text. They are included in each equation. Only results for the electoral variables are presented.

level. What the electoral arrangements specification adds for us, above mere improvement in statistical fit, is knowledge about which types of electoral arrangements have impact.

The regression coefficients provide more supportive evidence. The high/high category reveals two electoral arrangement variables reaching statistical significance (party competition, at-large). Both have the correct signs. Further, their *b*'s are larger than for any of the other equations. This also holds for the insignificant length of term variable—its *b* in the high/high category is larger than or equal to its *b* in any other equation (it only reaches statistical significance in the low/low set). Only in the high/high case does the election dummy variable reach statistical significance (it does so strongly with a *t* value of –4.52).

Taken together, the results strongly speak to the improved statistical performance of the three-way conditional impact of electoral arrangements, bureaucratic resources, and public mobilization. Substantively, the results of the high/high electoral arrangements equation tell us that changing to an at-large election system decreases the relative payment of residents by 7 percent and that moving from the least to the most competitive state will lower relative residential prices by 29 percent. More reasonably, a 10 percent increase in competition will result in a 2.9 percent decrease in relative consumer prices.

This is not a fanciful level of change. Comparison of the Ranney (1976) scores with the Bibby (1983) scores for the states that elect their PUCs reveals some large increases in competition, shifts that Barrilleaux (1986) finds to be systematic and explicable. For instance, Louisiana changed by almost 12 percent on the indices, Montana by 7 percent, South Carolina by 9 percent, and Tennessee by 8 percent. That the range of the dependent variable can vary no more than from 0 to 1.00 mathematically, and actually varies only about 30 percent (from about 25 to 55), underscores the relative importance of these conditional effects. Thus, not only are the results meaningful in a statistical sense, but they are substantively meaningful as well. Under the proper conditions, the properly designed electoral institution can have policy impacts that the average voter should be able to detect. At least this is so for this policy.

Conclusions

Elections affect policy outcomes but only under certain conditions. For elections to lead to policies that the public rather than a special interest prefers, politicians must be exposed to possible defeat; the public must be mobilized or perceived to be so; and the policy-making institution must have the resources to assess public opinion, convert those opinions into policy options, and implement them. Results herein strongly support this multiple conditional effects perspective. In fact, when public mobilization and institutional resources are absent, the mere fact of election has no impact on policy (compare the election dummy equation with its baseline for the low/low set, Table 5.4). However, mobilizing the public, supplying the PUC with resources, while also exposing politicians to defeat, boosts the R^2 over the election dummy equation in the low/low set by 33 percent (from .52 to .85). Again, one can use an F test to compare the R^2 of two different equations. The F is 26.41, which is significant at the .01 level. Not only are these conditional effects present, they are of impressive magnitude.

We must be cautious about overstatement. Results also indicate that, at least in the realm of state telephone regulatory policy, elections alone do not determine policy. The regulatory environment is complex, and others—governors, legislators, and interest groups—can and do affect policy outcomes (see chapters 3 and 4). In this sense elections become but one of many forces affecting policy.

This study has not closed the book on electoral effects. Other questions remain unanswered. Do these effects generalize to other policy areas and other institutions? Although some states elect their PUC regulators, by and large, regulators and bureaucrats are not elected. Do the same conditions hold for legislatures, and if so, would they be of comparable magnitude? Might the "professional politician" be even more sensitive, creating even greater electoral effects? Further, as we found competitive effects important, does the decline of competition in congressional elections also signify a decline of congressional responsiveness to the public? Recent commentary seems to suggest Congress is more disposed toward serving special interests and Political Action Committees than the broader public, a view consistent with that forwarded here.

Moreover, we need to specify the electoral institution more fully. Are other features, such as nonpartisanship, important? Do different features of the institution interact with the environment or the type of issue, thereby promoting or retarding promulgation of policies that the public prefers? How might the technical complexity of an issue, even a mobilizing one, affect policy outputs? For instance, might technical complexity buffer against public pressures? (cf. Gormley, 1983).

What about the costs of electing regulators and bureaucrats? Is electing regulators desirable? Traditionally, one rationale for regulation has been to balance the financial requirements of public utilities with the needs of the public for affordable, nondiscriminatory access. Earlier generations of research, which asserted that the regulated captured their regulators (Bernstein, 1955), might find the election of regulatory commissioners to be a salutary way to frustrate capture. However, insofar as election may politicize the regulatory environment around public preferences, the financial solvency of regulated firms may be jeopardized. Unlike other policy areas, regulation was intended to ensure a proper balance between public and regulated interests. Upsetting that balance in either direction may lead to ill-conceived policy. While elections cannot overwhelm other influences, results suggest that when properly conditioned, elections can affect regulatory policy strongly. Consequently, public debate should consider not only how to make decision makers responsive to the public through election, but also whether electoral influences are desirable. As we might need to be reminded from time to time, the Founding Fathers were wary of too much democracy, and they might have been wise in that wariness.

Finally, we need to address the question of improperly designed electoral institutions. If voters are offered electoral controls, they will expect an impact on policy outcomes. At least, they will insist that elections provide more responsiveness to them than if elections were not held. However, if the election system is designed in such a way as

to frustrate responsiveness, a mismatch between symbolic and functioning institutions may result. When symbolic offerings of responsiveness are promised but the electoral institution cannot deliver, public
faith and confidence in elections can erode, and threats to the stability
and efficacy of the political system might ensue. Policy makers and
reformers should be cautioned when offering electoral reforms in the
hope of promoting public preferences over special-interest preferences. Improperly designed electoral reforms can alienate people. When alien-
ation toward elections arises, more demagogic, plebiscitary, and
direct-action styles of mass participation might be offered as a replacement.

Note

1. The mean and standard deviations for the dependent variable for the different breakdowns used in this and succeeding analyses are as follows:

	MEAN	STANDARD DEVIATION
Low Mobilization	.37	.04
High Mobilization	.38	.05
Low Bureaucratic Resources	.38	.04
High Bureaucratic Resources	.37	.05
Low Bureacratic Resources/Low Mobilization	.38	.06
High Bureaucratic Resources/Low Mobilization	.38	.05
Low Bureaucratic Resources/High Mobilization	.36	.05
High Bureaucratic Resources/High Mobilization	.37	.04

6

Conclusions

In this concluding chapter, I discuss two theoretical issues that my study has raised. The first concerns the nature of regulatory policy. The second relates to the nature of policy influence. First, however, I review the major findings and arguments made in this book.

Summary and Recapitulation of Findings

This study was presented in several parts. The first part, the introduction, presented the major idea, the conditional effects theory. Then chapters 1 and 2 used a historical approach to assess telephone regulation prior to divestiture. The last part, from chapters 3 to 5, statistically tested the conditional influence theories that were proposed as the major theoretical contributions of this work.

Chapter 1 discussed the origins of regulation from the creation of the telephone in 1876 to the implementation of the full federal regulatory regime in 1934, when the Federal Communications Commission was created. This chapter also presented some important theoretical elements that were utilized later on.

I presented a typology of public policies arrayed on a dimension of government involvement, from laissez-faire with its low level of government intercession, to nationalization, the ultimate in government control. In the case of the United States, I demonstrated how telecommunication policy, after government decided to participate actively, wavered between the two middle policy choices of antitrust and regulation. I also linked the debate between antitrust and regulatory policies to the competing ideas of economic efficiency and equity–universal service. This conceptual scheme and set of distinctions serve as a basis

for understanding the nature of the policy debate during the era sur-
rounding divestiture.

In chapter 1, I also developed another theoretical anchor, the multiple
interests perspective. In a detailed historical fashion, I showed how the
major interests came to be engaged in telecommunications regulation
by focusing on their interests and resource bases. Over time, AT&T,
along with the government and business and residential consumers of
telecommunications, came to view regulation as being in its best interest. Only AT&T's rivals, the independent telephone companies, balked
at this arrangement; but internal division among them, and the growing
public and political mood favoring regulatory intervention, forced their
acceptance of the regulatory regime as well.

Still, the policy that arose from the early history of government
involvement in telecommunications was a mixture of antitrust policies
and regulation. Antitrust policies were housed in the Antitrust Division
of the Department of Justice, which possessed some jurisdiction over
telecommunications policy. By not exempting AT&T from antitrust,
not only did the government enable independent telephone companies,
who preferred antitrust if there was to be a government policy, to win a
partial victory, but tensions between AT&T and the government arose
sporadically during the regulatory regime of 1933–84.

Chapter 2 resumes the historical discussion, which culminates in the
divestiture agreement in 1984. That chapter discussed in some detail
the economics of telephone pricing and how the federal and state governments erected the various cross-subsidies in pursuit of the universal
service–equity policy.

In particular, regulators insisted that since long distance calls had to
travel over the local loop to complete a call, every long distance call
was in part purely long distance and in part local. Thus, using this
station-to-station view, monies collected from long distance operations
were transferred to the local telephone companies. This became the
seed of the long distance-to-local cross-subsidy, which grew substan-
tially over the years. If a long distance vendor could bypass this local
"tax," the vendor could reap huge benefits by offering long distance
service at prices well below AT&T's. Huge profit potential also emanated from this service. This "loophole" in the regulatory scheme, plus
technological developments, created the window through which competitors (MCI in particular) could enter the market.

Chapter 2 also looked at the historic tension between AT&T and the

Antitrust Division of the Department of Justice and other advocates of the antitrust regime within the Federal Communications Commission. Several factors—the economic loophole, technological developments, MCI's attempts to enter the market, and a changing philosophy in the federal government away from regulation and toward antitrust (entirely consistent with the growing deregulation movement)—converged and reinforced one another, overwhelming AT&T, and resulting in divestiture.

Chapter 3 begins the empirical analysis of the effect of the subsystem participants on telephone rates. Carrying over the multiple interests perspective of the previous two chapters, I argued that public and private interests, state legislators and executives, and the regulatory bureaucrats themselves can all affect state telephone rate-making policy. The data employed consisted of a pooled cross sectional–time series covering the years 1977 through 1985.

Examination of rate trends over the years shows that states did not uniformly react to divestiture. Some increased rates to consumers, some maintained steady rates, and some even forced declines in rates. The variety of responses was expected to be a function of the impact of divestiture on the coalitions of interests that governed telephone rate-making policy in the several states.

Using regression techniques, I found that the ratio between urban residential and business rates declined when the legislature is controlled by Democrats, when the legislature holds strong oversight powers over the state public utility commissions, when the public utility commission is an arm of the executive branch, when Common Cause is more strongly represented in the state's population, and when the state displays a higher incidence of poverty. All of these factors work to the advantage of consumers, who prefer lower rates relative to business. In contrast, relative rates increase when the public utility commissions possess higher employee totals. Thus, as we argued all along, the political composition of a state greatly affects rate-making policy.

The argument of chapter 3, however, is theoretically deficient. It views rates as but a linear combination of forces. As I discussed in the introduction, the influence of actors on policy outcomes depends also on the level of resources of competing actors. Hence, there is an interaction among actors in the policy system that the linear, multiple regression model does not easily capture. This I labeled the *theory of relative resources*.

Chapter 4 refined the analysis to test that theory. The relative resources theory of policy influence is compared with its major competitors, interest group capture and the linear version of multiple interest influence, as presented in the previous chapter. In all tests the relative resources perspective beats its rivals.

Thus, rather than focusing on the actual level of resources that a policy actor may possess, the message of this analysis is that we should focus on the relative resources that an actor possesses. If an actor possesses considerable resources, that will translate into policy influence only if competitors do not possess comparable levels of resources. Undergirding the theory of relative resources is the pluralist notion of countervailing power.

Chapter 5 looked at another conditional impact, that of elections on rate policy. Often a neglected topic, the impact of the public on regulatory policy and bureaucratic decision making became apparent with the revolution in citizen participation at regulatory proceedings. Attendant with that revolution have been calls to elect regulators, with the hopes of increasing not only regulatory responsiveness to the public but accountability as well.

The theory and analysis presented in chapter 5, however, finds that simply changing to electoral recruitment may not affect policy outcomes. A conditional theory of election effects is offered, which focuses on the nature of electoral arrangements, the mobilization of the public, and the institutional resources of the elected body. All three acting in concert are required to promote responsiveness by elected regulators. This chapter has important reform as well as theoretical implications.

The next two sections of this concluding chapter relate these findings to two theoretical issues implicitly raised throughout the study: the nature of regulatory policy and the nature of policy influence.

The Nature of Regulatory Policy

The discussion of regulatory policy presented in this study focused on the debate between equitable and efficient regulatory policies. This view, with its focus on regulatory policy winners and losers, differs from the more common and popular approaches to understanding regulatory policy.

Perhaps the most influential view of regulation among political scientists is the one first elaborated by Theodore Lowi (1964, 1972).

Lowi's theory distinguishes among regulatory, distributive, and redistributive policy (constituent policy was added in the 1972 essay). Important in distinguishing among these policy types are the actors involved in making and implementing the policies, the government instruments used to implement the policies, and the degree and nature of conflict associated with each type of policy. Regulatory policy is usually described as being constructed within policy subsystems, in which Congress, especially its committees and subcommittees, and regulated interests are most active, while implementation responsibility typically resides with the bureaucracy. Moreover, conflict often runs high and government coercion is the instrument through which regulatory policy is implemented and enforced.

Although it has been seminal, scholars have rarely used Lowi's typology intact, in part because it does not discriminate among types of regulatory policies. To be fair, that was not Lowi's intention. Distinguishing among regulation, distribution, and redistribution itself is a contribution.

Several scholars have offered refinements that differentiate policy forms within the regulatory policy type. First, as Meier (1985, 2) argues, not all regulation is coercive. Many forms of regulation rely on inducements to alter behavior. Other regulatory policy distinctions focus on the substance of policy. Ripley and Franklin (1984, 1986) offer the distinction between competitive and protective regulatory policy; Gerston, Fraleigh, and Schwab (1988) contrast economic and social regulation; and White (1981) distinguishes between old and new regulation. Whatever one calls these substantive types of regulation— competitive versus protective, economic versus social, or old versus new—they all have several themes in common.

"Competitive-economic-old" forms regulate behavior within one sector of the economy, often limiting competition. The effect is usually to support or promote firms that are regulated, which is the reason that charges of interest group capture often arise as criticisms of these regulatory policies. In contrast, "protective-social-new" styles of regulation often impose regulation across the whole economy, frequently with the express purpose of protecting consumers, the average citizen, and so forth. The intent of such regulation is never to aid businesses, but the effectiveness of these regulations in protecting consumers is often open to debate.

While heuristically useful, these regulatory policy types are sometimes difficult to employ in more empirical analysis. For instance, they often fail to note the potential for conflict among regulated firms or that consumer and business interests are not always antagonistic. How, for instance, should we classify telephone policy under the universal service–equity regime? Clearly, AT&T benefited from that regime, but we can also argue that many consumers did. If consumers benefited, is the policy protective or competitive? It is both.

Moreover, none of the standard political science approaches to regulation appreciate the redistributive nature of regulation. Economists more often focus on the redistributive consequences of regulation. This is where the equity–efficiency dimension becomes useful (Stone, 1982).

Whether regulatory policy falls near the equity or efficiency poles determines to a large degree the nature of the resulting redistribution. Quite often, efficient regulatory policy solutions benefit businesses or firms that provide the regulated service. Less regard is paid to benefiting classes of consumers. Moreover, efficient policies sometimes benefit a subset of firms, while harming others. Generally, it may be fair to say that efficient policies redistribute toward the benefit of firms that provide regulated services and away from consumers—that efficient policies are distributionally regressive. When interest groups capture their regulators and policy is skewed strongly in their favor, the most extreme examples of regressive redistributions may be found. This also helps us understand the charges and criticisms of populist reformers.

Equitable regulatory policies, in contrast, redistribute in the other direction, toward consumers. Sometimes this type of regulatory policy harms some or all firms providing the service, thus suggesting a redistributional progressivity to equitable regulatory policies. When regulatory policy tilts toward equity goals, and in so doing becomes redistributionally progressive, it seems natural for regulated firms, or other firms with interests in the type of regulation, to push for the type of regulation that may better help them, efficient regulation.

The predivestiture regulatory regime aligned AT&T with consumers against big businesses, who increasingly came to utilize long distance for intracorporate communications as well as market transactions. Also, it seems that over the years of the equity–universal service regulatory regime, AT&T adopted a public service ethic, which we might speculate transformed the giant firm into a quasi-government bureaucracy.

Clearly, the nature of redistributions associated with regulation are quite complex, as regulated firms might be in different competitive positions; nonregulated firms, as consumers of regulated services, might stand in opposition to regulated firms, as well as disagreeing among themselves; and consumers might not be monolithic, as regulation differentially benefits classes of consumers. AT&T and its major competitors in the end of the equity regime, MCI and Sprint, sought different regulatory regimes. Big and small business had different interests concerning the course of telecommunications regulation. And urban and rural folk had divergent interests. Regulation involves many subtle conflicts.

Perhaps the chief advantage of viewing regulation from the equity-efficiency debate is that one can view regulatory policy more dynamically. Neither the Lowi orientation, nor the "competitive-economic-old" and "protective-social-new" regulatory approaches allows for dynamism in regulatory policy. And clearly the deregulations of the last 15 years starkly reveal the potential for change within regulatory regimes. My point is not that we should view regulation solely from the equity–efficiency perspective, but that our understanding of regulatory policy is enriched when we appreciate the redistributional consequences of regulation.

The Nature of Policy Influence

All theories of regulatory policy outcomes are theories of influence. In this book, I have tried to propose a direction for studying influence in the regulatory policy process. That direction builds upon Robert Dahl's (1957, 1968) work on power and influence, but it goes beyond Dahl with the suggestion, not inconsistent with Dahl, that influence in the policy-making process is conditional.

I specified two important conditions to the exercise and effectuation of policy-making influence: the idea of relative resources and the efficiency of the translation of resources into influence. Undergirding the argument is the view that resources serve as the foundation upon which influence is built. Thus, I spent much time discussing not only the conditional nature of influence but also the nature of resources. Throughout, I argued that the ability to utilize information, which usually meant possessing the organizational capability to manipulate information, plus possessing political supporters (e.g., voters, politicians) that no one else can claim, were fundamental resource building blocks.

These resources blocks (or assets), however, are situated within a context that conditions how potent or influential those resources will be, and relates to the number and resourcefulness of one's policy competitors. I called this notion *relative resource conditions*.

Relative Resource Conditions

The relative resources idea is especially useful for explaining outcomes in a context of multiple actors. The relative resources theory suggests that it is not the level of resources that one commands that is important for policy influence. Rather, it is the level of resources compared to one's policy competitors, whether one possesses a resource advantage or disadvantage, that is important for policy influence. As such it coincides well with the now-common view among political scientists that regulatory policy making involves the participation of a number of interested parties, including but not limited to interest groups, public interest groups, legislators, executives, bureaucrats, and the mass public. This multiple interest view contrasts sharply with the venerable interest group capture theory, which holds that only interest groups were important to understanding regulatory policy decision making, a view still popular among economists (see the review in Meier, 1988, 18–32).

The most important theoretical attribute of the relative resources idea is that it explains more situations than its major theoretical rivals, interest group capture or absolute resources. Absolute resources theory suggests that influence is based on the amount of resources at one's disposal. Such a version of multiple-actor influence does not model the interactions of the resources of the competing actors, the foundation of the relative resources theory.

Further, not only is the relative resources idea broader than interest group capture or absolute resource theories, it also suggests predictions about policy influence that differ from those that capture or absolute resources theories advance. These contrasting hypotheses and propositions are testable and were tested in what we may take as critical experiments. Results supported the relative resources notion as opposed to capture or absolute resources.

Relative resources may also be taken as a way to integrate theories of influence, such as Dahl's, with theories of countervailing power (McFarland, 1987). In this view of countervailing power, we need not envision a system in balance or equilibrium. Rather, we need only recognize the competition among actors for policy influence and that this competition implies interaction.

The basis of relative resource interaction is that policy competitors cancel out one another's resource base; the actor with the greater net reserves of resources will have the greater net impact on policy outcomes. Important in this theory is that it is not the absolute amount of resources that leads to policy influence but only the relative amount. Thus, objectively resourceful groups may have minimal policy influence because they are opposed by similarly resourceful competitors.

Another way in which the relative resources idea is useful is that more than just interest groups can be conceptualized as having policy influence. Applying this to notions of countervailing power leads us away from archaic versions of pluralism, which viewed government as but the arbiter of interest group conflict (e.g., Fainsod, 1940). Government, rather, becomes a party to policy conflict and debate.

Consistent with the work of Teske (1990, 1991) on telecommunication regulation in the states, we find that political institutions affect policy outcomes, and on the whole appear more influential than interest groups. In fact, it is quite striking that among AT&T, a state's business community, and ties between regulators and regulated, none seemed to affect the residential/business rate ratio. In contrast, legislatures and governors did, as did the public utility commissions themselves.

How Resources Translate into Influence

The second condition looks at how political structures and arrangements translate resources into influence. The general point here is that some political structures translate resources into influence more efficiently than others. Efficient translation entails not only matching the resource to the political structure, but also being able to take advantage of properly matched resources.

I focused on the impact of electoral structures. While votes are a key electoral resource that the public possesses, for the public to use its votes efficiently, electoral systems have to be designed to maximize the impact of votes. Not all electoral systems do this. Vote impact on policy outcomes rises (becomes more efficient) the more that elections affect the representative's security in office. If elected politicians feel insecure in their ability to retain office, their responsiveness to the public will increase. The less insulated election-based political careers are from the public, the more efficient the electoral institution is in translating public preferences into policy outcomes. Competitiveness, short terms of office, and higher turnout rates all expose electorally based careers.

Elections also seem to have greater impact when the body for which elections are held possesses the institutional resources to influence the policy-making process. Feebly endowed public utility commissions, even under electorally vulnerable situations, may be less able to promote public preferences into policy than their well-endowed counterparts, not because of lack of desire, but because of lack of capability. Public control of policy is enhanced when democratic institutions are strong rather than weak.

This point also resonates sharply with the relative resources notion. If we aim to foster public control over public policy, a lofty but requisite aim of all democratic systems, then those democratic institutions must be strong and preferably stronger than bureaucratic institutions. Hopefully, the ideas and findings presented in this study will take us further in understanding the specific implications of that point.

References

Amacher, Ryan C., and William J. Boyes. 1978. "Cycles in Senatorial Voting Behavior," *Public Choice*, 33:5–13.

American Telephone and Telegraph Company. 1914. *Government and Private Telegraph Utilities: An Analysis*, reprinted in abridged form in K. Judson, ed. *Selected Articles on Government Ownership of the Telegraph and Telephone*. White Plains, NY: H. W. Wilson, pp. 129–57.

Anonymous. 1939. "Direct Regulation of the American Telephone and Telegraph Company," *Yale Law Journal*, 48:1015–35.

Arnold, R. Douglas. 1979. *Congress and the Bureaucracy: A Theory of Influence*. New Haven: Yale University Press.

Barnett, William P., and Glenn R. Carroll. 1987. "Competition and Mutualism Among Early Telephone Companies," *Administrative Science Quarterly*, 32:400–21.

Barrilleaux, Charles B. 1986. "A Dynamic Model of Partisan Competition in the American States," *American Journal of Political Science*, 30:822–40.

Bernstein, Marver. 1955. *Regulating Business by Independent Commission*. Princeton, NJ: Princeton University Press.

Bernstein, Robert A. 1988. "Do U.S. Senators Moderate Strategically?" *American Political Science Review*, 82:237–41.

Berry, William. 1979. "Utility Regulation in the States: The Policy Effect of Professionalism and Salience to the Consumer," *American Journal of Political Science*, 23:263–77.

Bethel, Frank H. 1914. "Some Comments on Government Ownership of Telephone Properties," in K. Judson, ed. *Selected Articles on Government Ownership of the Telegraph and Telephone*. White Plains, NY: H. W. Wilson, pp. 159–62.

Beyle, Thad. 1983. "Governors," in V. Gray, H. Jacob, and K. Vines, eds. *Politics in the American States*, 4th ed. Boston: Little, Brown, pp. 180–221.

Bibby, John F., et al. 1983. "Parties in State Politics," in V. Gray, H. Jacob, and K. Vines, eds. *Politics in the American States*, 4th ed. Boston: Little, Brown, pp. 59–96.

Bickers, Kenneth. 1986. "The Problem of Governance and Institutional Change in the American Telecommunications Industry, 1876–1984," paper presented for the 1986 Conference Group on Political Economy in conjunction with the American Political Science Association.

Bolling, George H. 1983. *AT&T: Aftermath of Antitrust*. Washington, DC: National Defense University.

Bornholz, Robert, and David S. Evans. 1983. "The Early History of Competition in the Telephone Industry," in David S. Evans, ed. *Breaking Up Bell: Essays on Industrial Organization and Regulation*. New York: North-Holland, pp. 7–40.

Brooks, John. 1976. *Telephone: The First Hundred Years*. New York: Harper and Row.

Brooks, Sydney. 1914. "Public Ownership Abroad," in K. Judson, ed. *Selected Articles on Government Ownership of the Telegraph and Telephone*. White Plains, NY: H. W. Wilson. pp. 176–82.

Bryner, Gary. 1987. *Bureaucratic Discretion: Law and Policy in Federal Regulatory Agencies*. New York: Pergamon Press.

Bunce, Valerie. 1981. *Do New Leaders Make a Difference? Executive Succession and Public Policy Under Capitalism and Socialism*. Princeton, NJ: Princeton University Press.

Bureau of the Census, Department of Commerce. 1915. *Telephones and Telegraphs and Municipal Electric Fire-Alarm and Police-Patrol Signalling Systems, 1912*. Washington, DC: Government Printing Office.

Burns, James MacGregor. 1978. *Leadership*. New York: Harper and Row.

Carmines, Edward. 1974. "The Mediating Influence of State Legislatures on the Linkage Between Interparty Competition and Welfare Policies," *American Political Science Review*, 68:1118–24.

Chubb, John E. 1985. "The Political Economy of Federalism," *American Political Science Review*, 79:994–1015.

———. 1988. "Institutions, the Economy, and the Dynamics of State Elections," *American Political Science Review*, 82:133–54.

Clark, W. 1892. "Telegraph and Telephone Properly Parts of the Post Office System," *Arena*, March: 464–71.

Cohen, Jeffrey E. 1986. "The Dynamics of the 'Revolving Door' on the FCC," *American Journal of Political Science*, 30:689–708.

Coll, Steve. 1986. *The Deal of the Century: The Breakup of AT&T*. New York: Touchstone.

Coon, Horace. 1939. *American Tel and Tel: The Story of a Great Monopoly*. New York and Toronto: Longmans, Green (reprinted in 1971, Freeport, NY: Books for Libraries Press).

Costello, Kenneth. 1984. "Electing Regulators: The Case of Public Utility Commissions," *Yale Journal of Regulation*, 2:83–105.

Dahl, Robert A. 1957. "The Concept of Power," *Behavioral Scientist*, 2:201–15.

———. 1968. "Power," *International Encyclopedia of the Social Sciences*. New York: MacMillan and Free Press, vol. 12, pp. 405–15.

Danielian, N. R. 1939. *AT&T: The Story of Industrial Conquest*. New York: Vanguard Press.

Dawson, Richard E., and James A. Robinson. 1963. "Interparty Competition, Economic Variables, and Welfare Politics in the American States," *Journal of Politics*, 25:265–89.

Denzau, Arthur T., and Michael C. Munger. 1986. "Legislators and Interest Groups: How Unorganized Interests Get Represented," *American Political Science Review*, 80:89–106.

Derthick, Martha, and Paul Quirk. 1985. *The Politics of Deregulation.* Washington: Brookings.

Dougan, William R., and Michael C. Munger. 1989. "The Rationality of Ideology," *Journal of Law and Economics*, 32:119–42.

Du Boff, Richard B. 1984. "The Rise of Communication Regulation: The Telegraph Industry, 1844–1880," *Journal of Communication*, 34:52–65.

Dubois, Philip L. 1980. *From Ballot to Bench.* Austin: University of Texas Press.

Dye, Thomas R. 1966. *Politics, Economics and the Public.* Chicago: Rand McNally.

Elling, Richard C. 1982. "Ideological Change in the United States Senate: Time and Electoral Responsiveness," *Legislative Studies Quarterly*, 7:75–92.

Elzinga, Kenneth G. 1970. "Predatory Pricing: The Case of the Gunpowder Trust," *Journal of Law and Economics*, 13:223–40.

Engstrom, Richard L., and Michael E. McDonald. 1981. "The Election of Blacks to City Councils: Clarifying the Impact of Electoral Arrangements on the Seats/Population Relationship," *American Political Science Review*, 75:344–54.

Ethridge, Marcus. 1981. "Legislative-Administrative Interaction as 'Intrusive Access': An Empirical Analysis," *Journal of Politics*, 43:473–92.

Eulau, Heinz, and Paul D. Karps. 1978. "The Puzzle of Representation: Specifying Components of Responsiveness," in H. Eulau and J. C. Wahlke, eds. *The Politics of Representation: Continuities in Theories and Research.* Beverly Hills, CA: Sage, pp. 55–71.

Evans, David S., ed. 1983. *Breaking Up Bell: Essays on Industrial Organization and Regulation.* New York: North-Holland.

Fainsod, Merle. 1940. "Some Reflections on the Nature of the Regulatory Process," in Carl J. Friedrich and Edward S. Mason, eds. *Public Policy.* Cambridge, MA: Harvard University Press, pp. 297–323.

Federal Communications Commission. 1938. *Proposed Report: Telephone Investigation.* Washington, DC: Government Printing Office.

———. 1939. *Investigation of the Telephone Industry in the United States.* Washington, DC: Government Printing Office.

———. 1987. "Telephone Subscribership in the U.S.," Industry Analysis Division, September 8.

Fischer, Claude S. 1987. "Technology's Retreat: The Decline of Rural Telephony, 1920–1940," *Social Science History*, 11:295–327.

Gable, Richard. 1969. "The Early Competitive Era in Telephone Communication, 1983–1920," *Law and Contemporary Problems*, 34 (Spring):340–59.

Garnett, Robert W. 1985. *The Telephone Enterprise: The Evolution of the Bell System's Horizontal Structure, 1876–1909.* Baltimore: Johns Hopkins.

Gerston, Larry N., Cynthia Fraleigh, and Robert Schwab. 1988. *The Deregulated Society.* Pacific Grove, CA: Brooks-Cole.

Gilligan, Thomas W., William J. Marshall, and Barry R. Weingast. 1986. "A Reconsideration of the Railroad Problem: The Economics and Politics of the Interstate Commerce Act," Working Papers in Political Science P–86–4, Hoover Institution, Stanford University.

Gormley, William. 1979. "A Test of the Revolving Door Hypothesis at the FCC," *American Journal of Political Science*, 23:665–83.

———. 1983. *The Politics of Public Utility Regulation*. Pittsburgh: University of Pittsburgh Press.

Grumm, John. 1969. "The Effects of Legislative Structure on Legislative Performance," in R. Hofferbert and I. Sharkansky, eds. *State and Urban Politics*. Boston: Little, Brown, pp. 307–22.

Hagerman, Robert, and Brian Ratchford. 1978. "Some Determinants of Allowed Rates of Return on Equity to Electric Utilities," *Bell Journal of Regulation*, 9:46–55.

Harris, Malcolm, and Peter Navarro. 1983. "Does Electing Public Utility Commissioners Bring Lower Electric Rates," *Public Utilities Fortnightly*, 112:23–28.

Henck, Fred W., and Bernard Strassburg. 1988. *A Slippery Slope: The Long Road to the Breakup of AT&T*. New York: Greenwood.

Herring, James M., and Gerald C. Gross. 1936. *Telecommunications: Economics and Regulation*. New York: McGraw-Hill.

Hofferbert, Richard I. 1966. "The Relationship Between Public Policy and Some Structural and Environmental Variables in the American States," *American Political Science Review*, 60:73–82.

Holcombe, Arthur N. 1914. "Public Ownership of Telegraphs and Telephones," *Quarterly Journal of Economics*, 28:581–656.

Holmes, Fred L. 1915. *Regulation of Railroad and Public Utilities in Wisconsin*. New York: D. Appelton.

Holmes, George K. 1890. "State Control of Corporations and Industry in Massachusetts," *Political Science Quarterly*, 5:411–37.

Horwitz, Robert Britt. 1986. "For Whom the Bell Tolls: Causes and Consequences of the AT&T Divestiture," *Critical Studies in Mass Communications*, 3:111–54.

Isaac, R. Mark, and Vernon L. Smith. 1985. "In Search of Predatory Pricing," *Journal of Political Economy*, 93:320–45.

Judson, Katherine B. 1914. *Selected Articles on Government Ownership of the Telegraph and Telephone*. White Plains, NY: H. W. Wilson.

Kahaner, Larry. 1986. *On the Line*. New York: Warner.

Kahn, Alfred. 1984. "The Road to More Intelligent Telephone Pricing," *Yale Journal of Regulation*, 1:139–57.

Kahn, Alfred, and William Shew. 1987. "Current Issues in Telecommunications Regulation: Pricing," *Yale Journal of Regulation*, 4:191–257.

Kaserman, David L., and John W. Mayo. 1986. "The Ghosts of Deregulated Telecommunications: An Essay By Exorcists," *Journal of Policy Analysis and Management*, 6:84–109.

Kau, James, and Paul Rubin. 1982. *Congressmen, Constituents, and Contributors*. Boston: Martinus Nijhoff.

Key, V. O. 1949. *Southern Politics in State and Nation*. New York: Vintage.

Kingdon, John. 1974. *Congressmen's Voting Decisions*. New York: Harper and Row.

Koller, Ronald H. 1971. "The Myth of Predatory Pricing: An Empirical Study," *Antitrust Law and Economic Review*, 5:105–23.

Kraus, Constantine Raymond, and Alfred W. Duerig. 1988. *The Rape of Ma Bell: The Criminal Wrecking of the Best Telephone System in the World.* Secaucus, NJ: Lyle Stuart.

Krislov, Samuel, and David H. Rosenbloom. 1981. *Representative Bureaucracy and the American Political System.* New York: Praeger.

Kuklinski, James H. 1978. "Representativeness and Elections: A Policy Analysis," *American Political Science Review*, 72:165–77.

Langdale, John V. 1978. "The Growth of Long Distance Telephony in the Bell System, 1875–1907," *Journal of Historical Geography*, 4:145–59.

Lineberry, Robert L., and Edmund P. Fowler. 1967. "Reformism and Public Policies in American Cities," *American Political Science Review*, 61:701–16.

Lipartito, Kenneth. 1988. "The Telephone in the South: A Comparative Analysis, 1877–1920," *Journal of Economic History*, 48:419–21.

———. 1989. "System Building at the Margin: The Problem of Public Choice in the Telephone Industry," *Journal of Economic History*, 49:323–36.

Long, Norton. 1937a. "Public Relations of the Bell System," *Public Opinion Quarterly*, 1:5–22.

———. 1937b. "Public Relations of the Bell System," Ph.D. dissertation, Harvard University.

———. 1962. "Popular Support for Business Policy: The Bell System as a Case Study," in N. Long, ed. *The Polity.* Chicago: Rand McNally.

Lowi, Theodore J. 1964. "American Business, Public Policy, Case Studies, and Political Theory," *World Politics*, 16:677–715.

———. 1972. "Four Systems of Policy, Politics, and Culture," *Public Administration Review*, 32:298–310.

MacAvoy, Paul W., and Kenneth Robinson. 1983. "Winning By Losing: the AT&T Settlement and Its Impact on Telecommunications," *Yale Journal of Regulation*, 1:1–42.

———. 1985. "Losing By Judicial Policymaking: The First Year of the AT&T Divestiture," *Yale Journal of Regulation*, 2:225–62.

MacMeal, Harry B. 1934. *The Story of Independent Telephony.* Chicago: Independent Pioneer Telephone Association.

McCloskey, Herbert, and John Zaller. 1984. *The American Ethos: Public Attitudes toward Capitalism and Democracy.* Cambridge, MA: Harvard University Press.

McFarland, Andrew. 1984. *Common Cause: Lobbying in the Public Interest.* Chatham, NJ: Chatham House.

McFarland, Andrew S. 1987. "Sources of Countervailing Power in America: Contributions from Recent Interest Group Theory," paper delivered at the meeting of the American Political Science Association, Chicago, Illinois, September 3–6.

Mann, Patrick, and Walter Primeaux. 1983a. "The Controversial Question of Commissioner Selection," *Public Utilities Fortnightly*, 111:21–25.

———. 1983b. "Elected Versus Appointed Commissioners: Does it Make a Difference in Utility Prices?" in H. Trebing, ed. *Adjusting to Regulatory Pricing and Market Realities.* East Lansing, Michigan: Institute of Public Utilities, Graduate School of Business Administration, Michigan State University, pp. 56–72.

Meier, Kenneth J. 1980. "Measuring Organizational Power: Resources and Autonomy of Government Agencies," *Administration and Society*, 12:357–75.

———. 1985. *Regulation: Politics, Bureaucracy, and Economics*. New York: St. Martins.

———. 1987. *Politics and the Bureaucracy: Policymaking in the Fourth Branch of Government*, 2d ed. Monterey, CA: Brooks-Cole.

———. 1988. *The Political Economy of Regulation: The Case of Insurance*. Albany, NY: SUNY Press.

Mitnick, Barry. 1980. *The Political Economy of Regulation*. New York: Columbia University Press.

Mladenka, Kenneth R. 1989. "Blacks and Hispanics in Urban Politics," *American Political Science Review*, 83:165–91.

Moe, Terry. 1985. "Control and Feedback in Economic Regulation: The Case of the NLRB," *American Political Science Review*, 79:1094–1116.

———1987. "An Assessment of the Positive Theory of 'Congressional Dominance'," *Legislative Studies Quarterly*, 12:475–520.

Mosher, William E. 1935. "Public Utilities and Their Early Regulation," in Alexander C. Flick, ed. *History of the State of New York in Ten Volumes*. New York: New York State Historical Association, vol. 8.

Nagel, Stuart S. 1973. *Comparing Elected and Appointed Judicial Systems*. Beverly Hills, CA: Sage.

NARUC. 1911. *Proceedings*. Washington, DC: National Association of Regulatory Utility Commissioners.

———. 1977–85a. *Annual Report on Utility and Carrier Regulation*. Washington, DC: National Association of Regulatory Utility Commissioners.

———. 1977–85b. *Exchange Service Telephone Rates*. Washington, DC: National Association of Regulatory Utility Commissioners.

National Civic Federation. 1913. *Commission Regulation of Public Utilities: A Compilation and Analysis of Laws of Forty-three States and of the Federal Government for the Regulation by Central Commissions of Railroads and Other Public Utilities*. New York: National Civic Federation, Department on Regulation of Interstate and Municipal Utilities.

Navarro, Peter. 1981. "Electric Utility Regulation and National Energy Policy, *Regulation*, Jan./Feb.: 20–27.

New York Times. 20 December 1908. "Federal Control of Telephones," p. 16.

———. 11 July 1909. "Plan Big Telephone Merger," p. 3.

———. 15 July 1909. "Competition Really Hurts," p. 9.

Nice, David, and Jeffrey Cohen. 1979. "Comment on LeLoup." *American Political Science Review*, 73:547–49.

Pelsoci, Thomas. 1979. "Organizational Correlates of Utility Rates," in Michael Steinman, ed. *Energy and Environmental Issues*. Lexington, MA: Lexington Books, pp. 101–16.

Peltzman, Sam. 1976. "Toward a More General Theory of Regulation," *Journal of Law and Economics*, 19:211–40.

Pindyck, Robert S., and Daniel L. Rubinfeld. 1981. *Econometric Models and Economic Forecasts*, 2d ed. New York: McGraw-Hill.

Pitkin, Hanna Fenichel. 1967. *The Concept of Representation*. Berkeley, CA: University of California Press.

Plotnick, Robert D., and Richard F. Winters. 1985. "A Politicoeconomic Theory of Income Redistribution," *American Political Science Review*, 79:458–73.

Pool, Ithiel de Sola. 1984. "Competition and Universal Service: Can We Get There From Here?" in Harry M. Shooshan III, ed. *Disconnecting Bell: The Impact of the AT&T Divestiture*. New York: Pergamon, pp. 112–31.

Posner, Richard A. 1974. "Theories of Economic Regulation," *Bell Journal of Economics and Management Science*, 5:335–58.

Ranney, Austin. 1976. "Parties in State Politics." In Herbert Jacob and Kenneth N. Vines, eds. *Politics in the American States: A Comparative Analysis*, 3d ed. Boston: Little, Brown, pp. 51–92.

Ripley, Randall B., and Grace A. Franklin. 1984. *Congress, the Bureaucracy, and Public Policy*, 3d ed. Homewood, IL: Dorsey Press.

———. 1986. *Policy Implementation and Bureaucracy*, 2d edition. Chicago, IL: Dorsey Press.

Robinson, Theodore P., and Thomas R. Dye. 1978. "Reformism and Black Representation on City Councils," *Social Science Quarterly*, 59:133–41.

Rourke, Francis. 1969. *Bureaucracy, Politics, and Public Policy*. Boston: Little, Brown.

Scholz, John, and Feng Heng Wei. 1986. "Regulatory Enforcement in a Federalist System," *American Political Science Review*, 71:1026–43.

Sharkansky, Ira, and Richard I. Hofferbert. 1969. "Dimensions of State Politics, Economics, and Public Policy," *American Political Science Review*, 63:867–80.

Sichter, James W. 1977. "Separations Procedures in the Telephone Industry: The Historical Origins of a Public Policy," Harvard University, Program on Information Resources Policy, P–77–2.

Smith, George David. 1985. *The Anatomy of a Business Strategy: Bell, Western Electric, and the Origins of the American Telephone Industry*. Baltimore: Johns Hopkins.

Soloman, Richard Jay. 1978. "What Happened After Bell Spilled the Acid? Telecommunications History: A View Through the Literature," *Telecommunications Policy*, 2:146–57.

State of New York. 1910. *Documents of the Senate of the State of New York*. 133d Sess., vol. 23, no. 37, part I.

Stehman, Warren J. 1925. *The Financial History of the American Telephone and Telegraph Company*. Boston: Houghton-Mifflin.

Stigler, George. 1971. "The Theory of Economic Regulation," *Bell Journal of Economics and Management Science*, 2:3–21.

Stimson, James. 1985. "Regression in Space and Time," *American Journal of Political Science*, 29:914–47.

Stone, Alan. 1982. *Regulation and Its Alternatives*. Washington, DC: CQ Press.

———. 1989. *Wrong Number: The Breakup of AT&T*. New York: Basic Books.

Temin, Peter, and Geoffrey Peters. 1985a. "Cross Subsidization in Telephone Network," *Willamette Law Review*, 21:199–223.

———. 1985b. "Is History Stranger than Theory? The Origin of Telephone Separations," *American Economic Review: Papers and Proceedings*, 75:326.

Temin, Peter, with Louis Galambos. 1987. *The Fall of the Bell System*. Cambridge, MA: Cambridge University Press.

Teske, Paul Eric. 1990. *After Divestiture: The Political Economy of State Telecommunications Regulation.* Albany, NY: SUNY Press.

Teske, Paul. 1991. "Interests and Institutions in State Regulation," *American Journal of Political Science,* 35:139–54.

Thomas, Martin. 1985. "Election Proximity and Senatorial Roll Call Voting," *American Journal of Political Science,* 29:96–111.

Unsigned. 1914. *Saturday Evening Post.* 18 April. "The Lame Duck," pp. 77–79.

Unsigned. 1914. "Telegraph and Telephone Prospects," *Journal of Political Economy,* 22:392–94.

Vedlitz, Arnold, and Charles A. Johnson. 1982. "Community Racial Segregation, Electoral Structure, and Minority Representation," *Social Science Quarterly,* 63:729–36.

Verba, Sidney, and Norman Nie. 1972. *Participation in America.* New York: Harper and Row.

Vietor, R., and D. Davidson. 1985. "Economics and Politics of Deregulation: The Issue of Telephone Access Charges," *Journal of Policy Analysis and Management,* 5:3–22.

von Auw, Alvin. 1983. *Heritage and Destiny.* New York: Praeger.

Wall Street Journal. 22 November 1974. "The Largest Antitrust Suit," p. 18.

Washington Post Weekly Edition. 9 January 1989. "The Polls," pp. 6–7.

Weingast, Barry, and Mark Moran. 1983. "Bureaucratic Discretion or Congressional Control? Regulatory Policymaking by the Federal Trade Commission," *Journal of Political Economy,* 91:765–800.

White, Lawrence J. 1981. *Reforming Regulation: Process and Problems.* Englewood Cliffs, NJ: Prentice-Hall.

Wilson, James Q., ed. 1980. *The Politics of Regulation.* New York: Basic.

Wood, B. Dan. 1988. "Principals, Bureaucrats, and Responsiveness in Clean Air Enforcements," *American Political Science Review,* 82:213–34.

Wright, Gerald C. 1976. "Linear Models for Evaluating Conditional Relationships," *American Journal of Political Science,* 20:349–73.

Wright, Gerald C., and Michael Berkman. 1986. "Candidates and Policy in United States Senate Elections," *American Political Science Review,* 80:567–90.

———. 1988. "Do U.S. Senators Moderate Strategically?" *American Political Science Review,* 82:241–45.

INDEX

Jeffrey E. Cohen received his Ph.D. in Political Science from the University of Michigan in 1979, and has served on the faculties of the Universities of Alabama, New Orleans, and Illinois before coming to the University of Kansas in 1992. He has authored articles on American government public policy in the major political science journals, including the *American Political Science Review* and the *American Journal of Political Science*. His first book, *The Politics of the U.S. Cabinet,* was published in 1988.